THE HERITAGE OF INDIA SERIES (8)

HYMNS FROM THE RIGVEDA

THE HERITAGE OF INDIA SERIES (8)

HYMNS FROM THE RIGVEDA

Selected and Metrically Translated

By

A. A. MACDONELL, M. A., PH.D., HON. LL. D.

GYAN

Published by

Gyan Publishing House
5, Ansari Road
Daryaganj, New Delhi-110002
Phone: 011-47034999, 9811692060
E-mail: books@gyanbooks.com

Distribution Network
gyanbooks.com
India, USA, Canada, UK, Australia, France

ISBN: 978-81-212-8270-3 (PB)
First Published, 1922

2nd Impression 2023

Printed at: Gyan Press, Delhi.

THE HERITAGE OF INDIA SERIES (8); HYMNS FROM THE RIGVEDA
TRANSLATOR: A. A. MACDONELL

THE HERITAGE OF INDIA SERIES

HYMNS FROM THE RIGVEDA

Selected and Metrically Translated

BY

A. A. MACDONELL, M.A., PH.D., HON. LL.D.

BODEN PROFESSOR OF SANSKRIT IN THE UNIVERSITY OF OXFORD
AND FELLOW OF BALLIOL COLLEGE.

ASSOCIATION PRESS
(Y.M.C.A.)
5, RUSSELL STREET, CALCUTTA

LONDON: OXFORD UNIVERSITY PRESS

PREFACE

This little book contains a selection of forty hymns from the *Rigveda*, translated in verse corresponding as nearly as is possible in English to the original metres. I have endeavoured to make the rendering as close as the use of verse will admit. Prose would have been more exact if I had had in view the requirements of linguistic students, but the general reader, to whom the spirit of the original hymns is the important thing, would have lost the means of appreciating, to some extent at least, the poetic beauty of the Vedic metres which form a considerable element in the literary charm of the hymns.

Although there are four Vedas, this selection of hymns has been made exclusively from the oldest and most important, the *Rigveda*. From it the other three have largely borrowed their matter, containing otherwise little that would be of interest in this selection.

The chief metres are here reproduced, and each of the most important gods is represented by at least one hymn. Of the comparatively few hymns not addressed to deities, I have also chosen a certain number dealing with cosmogony and eschatology, social life and magical ideas. This volume thus furnishes an epitome of the *Rigveda*, the earliest monument of Indian thought, the source from which the poetical and religious literature of India has in great part been derived and developed during a period of more than three thousand years.

The Introduction supplies a brief sketch of the form and contents of the *Rigveda*, enabling the reader to understand more fully the early thought of which these hymns are the outcome. There is, moreover, prefixed to each hymn a short account of the deity addressed or the subject dealt with. Without this supplementary aid, many notions of a mental atmosphere so far removed from those of our own time would be hardly intelligible. In the absence of footnotes, some passages may nevertheless seem obscure. Those who have any doubts as to the meaning of such may find it useful to refer to my *Vedic Reader* (Oxford, 1917), which supplies an exact prose rendering of about half the hymns in the present volume, together with full explanatory notes.

CONTENTS

INTRODUCTION

Of the four Vedas which constitute the earliest stage of Indian literature, the *Rigveda* is by far the most ancient and important. The exact period when its hymns were composed is a matter of conjecture. All that can be said is that the oldest of them cannot date from later than the thirteenth century B.C., because certain phases of literature subsequent to the Vedas are pre-supposed by Buddhism, which arose in the sixth century B.C. On the other hand, the most ancient part of the *Avesta*, which can hardly be older than 800 B.C., is linguistically very close to the *Rigveda*: it is therefore unreasonable to assume that the Indians separated from the Iranians more than 500 years earlier, or about 1300 B.C.

When the Indo-Aryans entered the north-west of India, they brought with them a religion in which the gods were mostly personified powers of nature. A few of these, such as Dyaus, "Heaven," and Uṣas, "Dawn," come down from Indo-European times; others, such as Mitra, Varuṇa, and Indra, from the Indo-Iranian age; while yet others were the creation of Aryans on Indian soil. They also brought with them the cult of fire and of Soma, as well as skill in composing religious poems in several metres. The purpose of these ancient hymns was to propitiate the gods by laudations that accompanied offerings of melted butter poured on the sacrificial fire and of the juice of the Soma plant deposited in vessels on the sacrificial grass. The hymns which have been preserved in the *Rigveda* from the early period of the Indo-Aryan invasion, were almost exclusively composed by a hereditary priesthood. They were handed down in different families by memory, not by writing, which can hardly have been introduced into India before 700 B.C. These family groups of hymns were gradually brought together till, with successive additions, they assumed the earliest collected form of the *Rigveda*. Then followed, about 600 B.C., the constitution of the Saṃhitā text, which did not in any way alter the wording of the collected hymns, but only subjected the text to certain euphonic rules prevalent at that time, by which vowels are either contracted or changed into semi-vowels, and the vowel *a* is often dropped, so that the metre is constantly obscured. Soon after this work was completed, extraordinary precautions were taken to preserve from corruption or loss the sacred text thus fixed. The earliest expedient of this kind was the Pada or "word" text, in which all the words of the Saṃhitā text are separated and given in their original form, unaffected by euphonic rules, and in which most compounds, as well as some derivatives and inflected forms, are analysed. This text, virtually the earliest commentary on the *Rigveda*, was followed by other and more complex methods of reciting the text, and by various Indexes, which enumerate the initial words of every hymn, stating the number of stanzas in each hymn, their deities and their metres, for the entire *Rigveda*. By these means the text of the *Rigveda* has been handed down for 2,500 years with a fidelity that is unparalleled in any other literature.

The *Rigveda* had 1,017 hymns with a total of about 10,600 stanzas, which give an average of slightly over 10 stanzas to each hymn. If printed continuously like prose in Roman characters, the Saṃhitā text would fill an octavo volume of 600 pages of 33 lines each. It has been calculated that the *Rigveda* is equal in bulk to the extant poems of Homer. The *Rigveda* is divided into ten books (*maṇḍala*, "cycle") and hymns (*sūkta*). This division is a historical one, which shows how the collection came into being. Of the ten books, six (ii-vii) are homogeneous in character, the hymns in each of them having been composed by poets of the same family.

The method of arrangement in these "family books" is uniform, each of them being similarly divided into groups addressed to different gods. On the other hand, books i, viii, and x were not each composed by a distinct family of seers, while the unity of the groups of which they consist depends on their being the work of different individual seers. Book ix differs from the rest by being addressed to one and the same deity, Soma, and by its groups being based on identity of metre, not of authorship. Internal evidence shows that the collection grew up in the following manner. The "family books" formed the nucleus. Then the second half of book i was prefixed; the eighth book was next placed at the end, and the first half of book i at the very beginning. The ninth book was formed by extracting all the Soma hymns from the family books, and all but three (which invoke Soma only in his general character), from books i and viii, and placing them as a collection for the use of the ritual Soma priest at the end of book viii. Book x was the final addition, both its language and its subject-matter showing that it is later than the other books. Moreover, both its position at the end and the fact that the number of its hymns (191) is brought up to that of book i, indicate its supplementary character.

The hymns of the *Rigveda* are composed in the earliest stage of that ancient literary language, of which the latest, or classical Sanskrit, was stereotyped by the grammar of Pāṇini at the end of the fourth century B.C. It differs from the latter about as much as Homeric from Attic Greek. It has a much greater variety of forms, especially in the verb, than Sanskrit. The language of the *Rigveda* also differs from Sanskrit in its accent, which, like that of ancient Greek, is of a musical nature, depending on the pitch of the voice, and is marked throughout the hymns. This accent has in Sanskrit been changed not only to a stress accent, but has shifted its position, depending now on quantity, and is no longer marked. The Vedic accent occupies a very important position in Comparative Philology, while the Sanskrit accent, being secondary, has no value of this kind. It may be affirmed with certainty that no student can understand Sanskrit historically without knowing the language of the Vedas.

The hymns of the *Rigveda* are without exception metrical. Their stanzas generally consist of four verses or lines, but also often of three and sometimes of five. The line, which forms the metrical unit, usually has eight, eleven, or twelve syllables. A stanza generally consists of lines of the same type; but some of the rarer metres are formed by combining lines of different length. The line has a quantitative rhythm in which short and long syllables alternate, being generally of the iambic type. Only the rhythm of the last four or five syllables of the line is rigidly determined, and the lines of eleven and twelve syllables have also a caesura, which comes after the fourth or the fifth syllable. The prevailing scheme of the octosyllabic line is: ⏓ – ⏓ – | ⏑ – ⏑ ⏓. That of the eleven syllable line is either (*a*) ⏓ – ⏓ –, ⏑ ⏑ – | – ⏑ – ⏓, or (*b*) ⏓ – ⏓ – ⏓, ⏑ ⏑ | – ⏑ – ⏓, the chief difference between these two being that the caesura comes after the fourth syllable in the former and after the fifth in the latter. This metre ends trochaically (– ⏑ – ⏑). The twelve-syllable line is similarly constructed, but, as it is extended by one syllable, it receives an iambic rhythm at the end (⏑ – ⏑ –). There are some fifteen metres, but only about seven of these are at all frequent. By far the most common are the Triṣṭubh (4 × 11 syllables), the Gāyatrī (3 × 8), and the Jagatī (4 × 12), which together furnish two-thirds of the total number of stanzas in the *Rigveda*. Usually a hymn of the *Rigveda* consists of stanzas in the same metre throughout. A typical departure from this rule is to mark the conclusion of a hymn with a stanza in a different metre.

The religion of the *Rigveda* is mainly concerned with the worship of gods that are largely personifications of the powers of nature. The hymns are predominantly invocations of these gods, being meant to accompany the oblation of Soma juice and the fire-sacrifice of melted butter. The religion of the Veda is thus essentially a polytheistic one, but it receives a pantheistic colouring in a few of the latest hymns of the *Rigveda*. The gods are stated to number thirty-three, a figure which, of course, does not include groups like the Maruts or Storm-gods. The gods are regarded as having had a beginning, but not as having all come into being at the same time; for earlier gods are occasionally referred to, and some deities are described as the offspring of others. They are considered to have been mortal at first; for they are said to have acquired immortality by drinking Soma or as a gift of Agni and Savitar. The gods are human in appearance. Their bodily parts are often merely illustrative of the phenomena of nature which they represent. Thus the tongue and the limbs of the fire-god, Agni, merely denote his flames. Some of the gods are warriors, especially Indra; others are priests, especially Agni and Bṛhaspati. All of them drive through the air in cars, drawn chiefly by horses, but sometimes by other animals. Their favourite food consists in milk, butter, grain, and the flesh of sheep, goats and cattle. They receive it in the sacrifice, which is either conveyed to them in heaven by Agni, or which they come in their cars to enjoy on the litter of grass prepared for them. Their favourite drink is the intoxicating juice of the Soma plant. Their abode is heaven, the third heaven, or the highest step of Viṣṇu, where, cheered by draughts of Soma, they live a life of bliss.

The most prominent attribute of the gods is power: they regulate the order of nature and overcome the mighty forces of evil; they hold sway over all creatures; no one can thwart their laws or live beyond the time they appoint; and the fulfilment of desires depends on them. The gods are also benevolent and bestow welfare on mankind, Rudra being the only one showing injurious traits. They are "true" and "not deceitful"; friends and protectors of the honest and righteous, but punishers of sin and guilt. As in most cases the gods of the *Rigveda* have not yet become detached from their physical basis, they are indefinite and lacking in individuality. Having many qualities, such as power, brilliance, benevolence, and wisdom, in common with others, each god has very few distinctive traits. This vagueness is increased by the practice of invoking deities in couples, when both gods share characteristics that properly belong to one alone. When nearly every quality can thus be ascribed to every god, the identification of one deity with another becomes easy. Several such identifications actually appear in the *Rigveda.* The idea even occurs in more than one late hymn, that various deities are but different forms of a single god. This idea, however, never developed into monotheism. Finally, in other late hymns we find the deities, Aditi and Prajāpati, identified not only with all the gods, but with nature as well. This brings us to the beginnings of that pantheism which became characteristic of later Indian thought in the form of the Vedānta philosophy.

The most convenient classification of the Vedic gods is in accordance with the threefold division of the universe, into heaven, air and earth, found in the *Rigveda* itself. The celestial deities are Dyaus, Varuṇa, Mitra, the Ādityas, Sūrya, Savitar, Pūṣan, Viṣṇu, the Aśvins, Uṣas and Rātrī. The deities of the atmosphere are Indra, Rudra, the Maruts, Vāyu or Vāta, Apāṃ Napāt, Parjanya, Āpas. The terrestrial deities are Pṛthivī, Agni, Bṛhaspati and Soma. Among these are included certain rivers, the Sindhu (Indus), the Vipāś (Bīas), the Śutudrī (Sutlej) and the Sarasvatī. All these are personified and invoked. The personfication goes farthest in the case of Sarasvatī, though the connexion of the goddess with the river is never lost sight of.

Alongside of the great nature gods there arose during the period of the *Rigveda* a class of abstract deities of two types. The first and earlier seems to have started from epithets which were applicable to one or more older deities, but which became detached and acquired an independent character as the want of a god exercising the particular activity in question began to be felt.

Some of these names denote an agent (formed with the suffix *tar*). Such is Dhātar, otherwise an epithet of Indra, appearing as an independent deity, the creator of heaven and earth, sun and moon. The only agent god of this kind at all often mentioned in the *Rigveda*, though never invoked in an entire hymn, is Tvaṣṭar, the "Artificer," the most skilled of workmen, who fashioned the bolt of Indra and a new drinking cup for the gods. A few other abstract deities, whose names, compound in form, originally epithets of older gods, represent the supreme god that was being evolved at the end of the Rigvedic period. These names are rare and late. The most important is Prajāpati, "Lord of Creatures." Originally an epithet of gods like Savitar and Soma, this name is employed in a late verse of the tenth book to designate a distinct deity in the character of a creator. Similarly, the epithet Viśva-karman, "all-creating," appears as the name of an independent deity to whom two hymns are addressed. The only abstract deity of this type occurring in the oldest as well as the latest hymns of the *Rigveda* is Bṛhaspati, the "Lord of Prayer."

The second and smaller class of abstract deities comprises personifications of abstract nouns. There are seven or eight of these, all found in the last book. Thus two hymns are addressed to Manyu, "Wrath," and one to Śraddhā, "Faith." The rest occur only in a few isolated passages. There is besides a purely abstract deity, often incidentally celebrated throughout the *Rigveda* as Aditi, "Freedom," whose main characteristic is the power of delivering from the bonds of physical suffering and moral guilt. She is the mother of the small group of deities called Adityas. These were, according to a common idiom, called the "Sons of Freedom," originally only in a figurative sense, which easily led to the personification of Aditi.

Goddesses play an insignificant part in the *Rigveda*. The only one of importance is Uṣas, "Dawn." Next comes Sarasvatī, the river goddess, and Vāc, "Speech," each invoked in two hymns. Pṛthivī, "Earth," Rātrī, "Night," and Araṇyānī, goddess of the forest, are each addressed in one hymn. Others are mentioned only in detached verses. The wives of the great gods are still more insignificant, lacking all individuality. They are mere names formed from those of their consorts, as Indrāṇī, "Wife of Indra."

A peculiar feature of the religion of the *Rigveda* is the invocation of pairs of deities, whose names are combined as compounds, each member being in the dual. About a dozen such pairs are invoked in entire hymns, and about a dozen more in detached stanzas. Mitrā-Varuṇā are addressed in by far the most hymns, though the names of this type oftenest mentioned are Dyāvā-Pṛthivī, "Heaven and Earth." The latter pair, having been associated as universal parents from the Indo-European period downwards, probably furnished the analogy for this dual type.

There are a few more or less definite groups of deities generally associated with some particular god. The Maruts, the attendants of Indra, are the most numerous group. The much smaller group of the Ādityas is constantly mentioned in company with their mother, Aditi. The Viśve devās, the "All-gods," invoked in about forty hymns, form a comprehensive sacrificial group, intended to include all the gods so that none should be left out; they are, strange to say, sometimes regarded as a narrower group, associated with other groups like the Ādityas.

Besides the higher gods, several lesser deities are known to the *Rigveda*. The most prominent of these are the Ṛbhus, who are invoked in eleven hymns. They are a deft-handed trio, who by their marvellous skill acquired the rank of deities. Among their five great feats of dexterity the greatest consisted in transforming the bowl of Tvaṣṭar into four shining cups. They further exhibited their skill in renewing the life of their parents, by whom heaven and earth seem to have been meant. A few of the lesser deities are of the tutelary order. Such is the rarely mentioned

Vāstoṣpati, "Lord of the Dwelling," who is invoked to grant a favourable entry, to remove disease, and to bestow protection and prosperity.

Besides the great phenomena of nature, various natural and artificial objects are found deified in the *Rigveda*. In addition to the rivers and waters already mentioned, mountains are often addressed as divinities, but only along with other natural objects, or in association with gods. One entire hymn is addressed to plants regarded as divine powers, chiefly with reference to their healing properties. Sacrificial implements are also deified, such as the sacrificial post, the sacrificial grass, and the "divine doors" leading to the sacrificial ground, the mortar and pestle used in pounding the Soma plant, and in three whole hymns the pressing stones, which are described as immortal, unaging, mightier than heaven, and driving away demons and destruction. Weapons, finally, are sometimes deified: armour, bow, quiver, arrows, and drum are invoked in one hymn.

Demons often appear in the *Rigveda*, and are of two kinds. The higher and more powerful are the aerial foes of the gods. The conflict is regularly one between a single god and a single demon, as exemplified by Indra and Vṛtra. The latter is by far the oftenest mentioned. Another powerful demon is Vala, the personified cave of the cows, which are set free by Indra. Other demon adversaries of Indra are Arbuda, a wily beast whose cows Indra drove out; Viśvarūpa, a three-headed demon slain by Indra, who seized his cows; and Svarbhānu, who eclipsed the sun. A group of demons are the Paṇis, primarily foes of Indra, who with the aid of Saramā tracked the cows concealed by them. The second or lower class of demons are terrestrial goblins, enemies of men. By far the commonest generic name for them is Rakṣas. They are nearly always mentioned in connexion with some god who destroys them. The much less frequent term Yātu or Yātu-dhāna (primarily "sorcerer") alternates with Rakṣas and perhaps expresses a species.

Some thirty of the hymns of the *Rigveda* are concerned with subjects other than the worship of gods or deified objects. About a dozen of these, almost entirely confined to the tenth book, deal with magical practices which properly belong to the sphere of the *Atharvaveda.* The contents of these are augury (ii, 42, 43), or spells directed against poisonous vermin (i, 191), or disease (x, 163), or a demon destructive of children (x, 162), or enemies (x, 166), or rival wives (x, 145); a few are propitious incantations: to preserve life (x, 58, 60), or to induce sleep (vii, 55), or to procure offspring (x, 183); while one is a panegyric of frogs as bringers of rain (vii, 103). Four hymns have a didactic character. One of these (x, 34) is a monologue in which a gambler laments the misery he has brought on himself and his home by his inability to resist the attraction of dice. The other three describe the various ways in which men follow gain (ix, 112), or praise wise speech (x, 71) and the value of good deeds (x, 117). Two hymns consist of riddles: one of these (viii, 29) describes various gods without mentioning their names; the other is more elaborate and obscure, being a long poem of 52 stanzas (i, 164) in which a number of enigmas, largely connected with the sun, are propounded in mystical and symbolic language. Thus the wheel of order with 12 spokes, revolving round the heavens and containing within it in couples 720 sons, means the year of 12 months with 360 days and 360 nights. Some half dozen are cosmogonic hymns, consisting of speculations on the origin of the world through the agency of a creator as distinct from any of the ordinary gods; one of them (x, 129) is particularly interesting as the starting point of the evolutionary philosophy represented in later times by the Sāṅkhya system. One complete hymn, and appendages of three to five stanzas attached to over thirty others, called Dānastutis or "Praises of gifts," have a semi-historical character as being panegyrics of liberal patrons on behalf of whom the seers composed their hymns. They yield incidental genealogical information about the poets and their patrons, as well as about the names and the habitat of the Vedic tribes.

Scattered incidentally throughout the *Rigveda* are to be found various geographical, historical, and social data throwing light on the life of the Indo-Aryans of those ancient days. Thus we can infer that the Vedic tribes, when the hymns were composed, occupied the territory more or less co-extensive with the North-West Frontier Province and the Panjab of to-day. They were still moving eastward as conquering invaders. Though divided into many tribes they were conscious of religious and racial unity, contrasting the aborigines with themselves by calling them non-sacrificers and unbelievers, as well as "black-skins" and the "Dāsa colour," as opposed to the "Ārya colour." Their food was mainly vegetarian; meat was eaten only when animals were sacrificed: the commonest kind appears to have been beef, as bulls were the chief offerings to the gods. Their main occupation was warfare: they fought either on foot or from chariots. Their ordinary weapons were bows and arrows, though spears and axes were also used. Cattle breeding seems to have been the main source of livelihood, cows being the principal object of desire in prayers to the gods. Agriculture was, however, also practised to some extent.

The literary merit of the *Rigveda* may, I think, be fairly well judged from the representative hymns contained in the present volume. Its diction is on the whole simple and natural. Considering their great antiquity, the hymns are composed with a surprising degree of metrical skill and command of language. But as they were produced by a sacerdotal class and were generally intended to accompany a ritual no longer primitive, their poetry is often impaired by constant sacrificial allusions. This is especially apparent in the hymns addressed to the two ritual deities, Agni and Soma, in which the thought becomes affected by conceits and obscured by mysticism. Neverthless the hymns contain much genuine poetry. The gods being mostly connected with natural phenomena, the praises addressed to them give rise to much beautiful and even noble imagery. The average level of literary merit is remarkably high. The most poetical hymns are those addressed to Dawn, which perhaps surpass in beauty the religious lyrics of any other literature. Some of the hymns to Indra show much graphic power in describing his conflict with the demon Vṛtra. The hymns to the Maruts, or Storm-gods, often depict with vigorous imagery the phenomena of thunder and lightning, and the mighty onset of the wind. The hymn to Parjanya (p. 52), paints with great vividness the devastating effects of the rain-storm. The hymns in praise of Varuṇa (p. 20) describe the various aspects of his sway, as moral ruler of the world, in an exalted strain of poetry. Some of the mythical dialogues set forth the situation with much beauty of language: for instance, the colloquy between Indra's messenger and the demons who drove off the cows (p. 94). The Gambler's Lament (p. 88) is a fine specimen of pathetic poetry. One of the funeral hymns (x, 18) expresses ideas connected with death (p. 86) in language of impressive and solemn beauty. One of the cosmogonic hymns (x, 129) illustrates (p. 19) how philosophical speculation can be clothed in poetry of no mean order.

CREATION

I. HYMN OF CREATION

X, 129. METRE : TRIṢṬUBH.

1. Non-being then existed not nor being :
   There was no air, nor sky that is beyond it.
   What was concealed ? Wherein ? In whose protection ?
   And was there deep unfathomable water ?

2. Death then existed not nor life immortal ;
   Of neither night nor day was any token.
   By its inherent force the One breathed windless :
   No other thing than that beyond existed.

3. Darkness there was at first by darkness hidden ;
   Without distinctive marks, this all was water.
   That which, becoming, by the void was covered,
   That One by force of heat came into being.

4. Desire entered the One in the beginning :
   It was the earliest seed, of thought the product.
   The sages searching in their hearts with wisdom,
   Found out the bond of being in non-being.

5. Their ray extended light across the darkness :
   But was the One above or was it under ?
   Creative force was there, and fertile power :
   Below was energy, above was impulse.

6. Who knows for certain ? Who shall here declare it ?
   Whence was it born, and whence came this creation ?
   The gods were born after this world's creation :
   Then who can know from whence it has arisen ?

7. None knoweth whence creation has arisen ;
   And whether he has or has not produced it :

He who surveys it in the highest heaven,
He only knows, or haply he may know not.

VARUṆA

The greatest of the gods of the *Rigveda*, beside Indra, is Varuṇa, though the number of hymns in which he alone (apart from Mitra) is addressed is only 12, as compared with the 250 to Indra. His physical features and activities are mentioned: he has face, eye, arms, hands and feet; he walks, drives, sits, eats and drinks. His eye, with which he observes mankind, is the sun. He sits on the strewn grass at the sacrifice. He wears a golden mantle or a shining robe. His car, drawn by well-yoked steeds, gleams like the sun. Varuṇa sits in his mansion surveying the deeds of men; and the Fathers behold him in the highest heaven. He has spies who sit around him and observe the two worlds. By his golden-winged messenger the sun is meant. He is often called a king, but especially a universal monarch. His sovereignty, his divine dominion, and his occult power (*māyā*) are specially emphasized. Varuṇa is characteristically an upholder of physical and moral order, the great maintainer of the laws of nature. He established heaven and earth, which he keeps asunder. He caused the sun to shine in heaven, and made for it a wide path. He placed fire in the waters and Soma on the rock. The wind that resounds through the air is his breath. By his ordinance the moon shining brightly moves at night, and the stars disappear by day. He is thus lord of light, both by day and by night. Varuṇa is also a regulator of the waters: he made the rivers flow; by his occult power they pour swiftly into the ocean without filling it. He is, however, more frequently connected with the atmospheric waters: thus he causes the inverted cask (the cloud) to shed its waters on heaven, earth and air, and to moisten the ground.

The fixity of his laws, which the gods themselves follow, is frequently mentioned. His power is so great that neither the birds as they fly, nor the rivers as they flow, can reach the limits of his dominion. His omniscience is typical: he knows the flight of the birds in the sky, the path of the ships in the ocean, the course of the far-travelling wind; he beholds all the secret things that have been or shall be done, and witnesses men's truth and falsehood; no creature can even wink without his knowledge.

Varuṇa is pre-eminent among the Vedic gods as a moral ruler. His anger is aroused by sin, which he severely punishes. The fetters with which he binds sinners are characteristic of him. But he is merciful to the penitent, releasing them from sin, even that committed by their fathers, and from guilt due to thoughtlessness. Every hymn addressed to Varuṇa contains a prayer for forgiveness of sin. Varuṇa is on a footing of friendship with his worshipper, who communes with him in his heavenly mansion, and sometimes sees him with his mental eye. The righteous hope to behold in the next world Varuṇa and Yama (the god of Death), the two kings who reign together in bliss.

Varuṇa seems originally to have represented the encompassing sky. But this conception has become obscured in the *Rigveda*, because it dates from a pre-Vedic period. It goes back to the Indo-Iranian age at least; for the Ahura Mazda, the "wise spirit" of the *Avesta*, agrees closely with the Asura (divine spirit) Varuṇa in character, though not in name. It may be even older, as *Varuṇa* is perhaps identical with the Greek οὐρανός, "sky." At any rate, the name appears to be derived from the root *vṛ*, to "cover" or "encompass."

II. VARUṆA

VII, 88. METRE: TRIṢṬUBH.

1. Present to Varuṇa the gracious giver
   A hymn, Vasiṣṭha, bright and very pleasant,
   That he may bring to us the lofty, holy
   And mighty steed that grants a thousand bounties.

2. Now having come to Varuṇa's full aspect,
   I think his countenance like that of Agni;
   May he, the lord, lead me to see the marvel:
   The light and darkness hidden in the cavern.

3. When Varuṇa and I the boat have mounted
And have propelled it to the midst of ocean;
When we shall move across the waters' ridges
We'll waver in the swing to raise its lustre.

4. Varuṇa has placed Vasiṣṭha in the vessel;
The sage benignant by his mighty power
His praiser in prosperity has settled,
As long as days endure, as long as mornings.

5. What has become of those our former friendships,
When we two held erstwhile unbroken converse?
O sovereign Varuṇa, thy lofty mansion,
Thy home, I entered, with its thousand portals.

6. Who is, O Varuṇa, thy constant kinsman,
Once dear, though sinful now, he claims thy friendships.
As guilty may we not, O wizard, suffer:
Do thou, O sage, grant shelter to thy praiser.

7. O may we, in these fixed abodes abiding,
Now from the lap of Aditi find favour.
May from his noose king Varuṇa release us.
Ye gods protect us evermore with blessings.

MITRA

Mitra is so intimately associated with Varuṇa that he is invoked alone in only one hymn of the *Rigveda*. The information about him in his separate capacity being so limited, his individual character is somewhat indefinite. He is the great Āditya (p. 26) who by his voice marshals men and watches the tillers with unwinking eye. That he is thought of as regulating the course of the sun is indicated by the fact that the solar deity Savitar (p. 32) is identified with him because of his laws, and another solar deity, Viṣṇu (p. 35), takes his three strides by the laws of Mitra. Agni (p. 69), who is kindled before dawn, is said to produce Mitra, and when kindled is identified with Mitra. In the *Atharvaveda* Mitra at sunrise is contrasted with Varuṇa in the evening, and in the Brāhmaṇas Mitra is associated with day, Varuṇa with night.

The Vedic evidence thus indicates that Mitra is a solar deity. This conclusion is confirmed by the cognate Iranian religion, in which Mithra is undoubtedly a sun-god.

The kindly nature of Mitra is often referred to in the Veda; the word also frequently means "friend" in the *Rigveda*, and in the *Avesta* Mithra is the guardian of faithfulness. The inference thus is that *mitra*, "friend," was originally a term applied to the sun-god in his capacity of a beneficent power of nature.

III. MITRA

III, 59. METRE: 1-5 TRIṢṬUBH; 6-9 GĀYATRĪ.

1. Mitra stirs men to action when he calls them;
Mitra supported both the Earth and Heaven;
Mitra with steady eye regards the people:
To Mitra offer now with ghee oblation.

2. Let him who, Mitra, brings thee food be foremost,
Who to thy law, O Āditya, pays homage.
Aided by thee no man is slain or vanquished;
To him from near or far no trouble reaches.

3. Free from disease, in sacred food delighting,
With knees set firm upon the earth's wide surface,
In this Āditya's sacred law abiding,
May we remain in the good will of Mitra.

4. This Mitra, worshippèd and most propitious,
Is born to wield fair sway, a king, disposer.
May we rest in the grace of him the holy,
May we abide in his most kindly favour.

5. The great Āditya to be served with homage,
Who stirs mankind, to singers most propitious:
To him most highly to be praised, to Mitra,
In fire present acceptable oblations.

6. The grace of Mitra, the divine
Supporter of mankind, brings gain
And splendour with most brilliant fame.

7. Mitra, whose fame is spread abroad,
In greatness who transcends the sky,
And in renown transcends the earth:

8. The peoples five submission yield
To Mitra ever strong to aid:
'Tis he who all the gods sustains.

9. Mitra, among both gods and men,
For him who strews the sacred grass
Has furnished food fixed by his will.

MITRA AND VARUṆA

These two gods are addressed as a pair in the dual more frequently than any other couple except Heaven and Earth. The hymns in which they are thus conjointly invoked are far more numerous than those in which they are separately addressed. As Mitra by himself (p. 23) has hardly any individual traits, the two gods together have practically the same attributes and functions as Varuṇa (p. 20) alone.

Mitra-Varuṇa are young and wear glistening garments. Their eye is the sun; they drive with the rays of the sun as with arms. They mount their car in the highest heaven. Their abode, which is golden, is located in heaven; it is great, very lofty, firm, with a thousand pillars and a thousand doors. They have spies who are wise and cannot be deceived. They are kings and universal monarchs, rulers and guardians of the whole world, who support heaven, air and earth. They are also called "divine spirits" (*asura*), who wield dominion by means of occult power. By that power they send the dawns, make the sun traverse the sky, and obscure it with cloud and rain.

They are lords of rivers, and they are the gods most frequently thought of and prayed to as bestowers of rain. One entire hymn dwells on their powers of granting rain. They control the rainy skies and the streaming waters. They send rain and refreshment from the sky. They bedew the pastures with ghee (*i.e.* rain) and the spaces with honey.

Mitra-Varuṇa are upholders and cherishers of order (*ṛta*). Their ordinances are fixed and cannot be infringed even by the immortal gods. They are barriers against falsehood, which they dispel, hate, and punish. They afflict with disease those who neglect their worship.

The dual worship of this divine pair goes back to the Indo-Iranian period, as Ahura and Mithra are thus coupled in the *Avesta.*

IV. MITRA AND VARUṆA

VII, 61. METRE : TRIṢṬUBH.

1. The beauteous eye of Varuṇa and Mitra,
The Sun, now rises up, his light extending,
Who with his gaze looks down upon all creatures:
He ever notes the burning zeal of mortals.

2. This pious priest, heard far away, here utters
His hymn for you, O Varuṇa and Mitra:
Do ye, O sages, treat his prayers with favour,
And may his autumns be replete with wisdom.

3. From wide-spread earth, O Varuṇa and Mitra,
Ye bounteous gods, and from the lofty heaven,
Ye have disposed your wandering spies in dwellings
And plants, ye who with watchful eye protect us.

4. Praise thou the law of Varuṇa and Mitra:
Their force the two worlds keeps with might asunder.
The months of impious men shall pass by sonless;
May those on worship bent increase their homestead.

5. Ye both are wise, O mighty ones, for you two
These lauds are sung without deceit or magic.
Avenging spies pursue men's falsehoods closely:
There are no secrets that ye cannot fathom.

6. With reverence I will consecrate your offering;
With zeal I call you, Varuṇa and Mitra.
These novel thoughts to praise you are intended:
May these the prayers that I have offered please you.

7. For you, O gods, this service has been rendered
At sacrifices, Varuṇa and Mitra.
Across all dangers do ye safely take us.
Ye gods protect us evermore with blessings.

THE ĀDITYAS

The group of gods called Ādityas is celebrated in six entire hymns of the *Rigveda* and in parts of two others. Their original number was seven, but in one passage of the last book, an eighth, Mārtāṇḍa (probably the setting sun) is added. In the *Atharvaveda* their number is eight. In the Brāhmaṇas it has grown to twelve; and in post-Vedic literature these are regularly twelve sun-gods connected with the twelve months. The names of the gods included in this group are not quite definite. Nowhere are more than six enumerated, and that only once: Mitra, Aryaman, Bhaga, Varuṇa, Dakṣa, Aṃśa. In a few passages Sūrya is called an Āditya, which is a common name of the sun in the Brāhmaṇas and later. He is therefore probably to be regarded as the seventh Āditya. Indra is, however, once coupled in the dual as an Āditya with Varuṇa, the chief of the Ādityas, and he is once directly invoked as the "fourth Āditya." When mention is made of one Āditya, it is generally Varuṇa; when of two, Mitra and Varuṇa; when of three, Varuṇa, Mitra, and Aryaman; when of five (which is only once the case), Varuṇa, Mitra, Aryaman, Bhaga, and Savitar. The Ādityas are often invoked as a group, when the names of Mitra and Varuṇa are generally mentioned at the same time.

The nature of the Ādityas as a class resembles that of the gods in general. In the aggregate sense they are the gods of celestial light, without representing any particular manifestation of that light. In some of the hymns in which the Ādityas are invoked, only the three most frequently mentioned together—Mitra, Varuṇa and Aryaman—seem to be meant.

The name of the Ādityas is a metronymic formation from that of their mother, Aditi, with whom they are naturally often invoked.

V. ĀDITYAS

II, 27. METRE : TRIṢṬUBH.

1. These songs that drip with butter, with the ladle
I ever to the kings, Ādityas, offer.
May Mitra, Aryaman, and Bhaga hear us,
Dakṣa, the mighty Varuṇa, and Aṃśa.

2. This praise of mine may Aryaman and Mitra
And Varuṇa to-day accept united :
The radiant Ādityas, like sword-blades shining,
From guile and falsehood free, unscathed, and blameless.

3. These Ādityas are deep and far-extending,
With many eyes, deceived not, but deceiving.
They look within, and see the straight and crooked.
Nigh to the kings is all, even what is farthest.

4. The Ādityas support what's fixed and moving ;
These gods are guardians of the whole creation :
Far-sighted, cherishing their spirit-power,
Observing holy law and guilt chastising.

5. May I, O Ādityas, meet with your favour,
Which even in danger, Aryaman, brings comfort.
Guided by you, O Varuṇa and Mitra,
May I avoid all troublous times, like pitfalls.

6. Smooth is your path, O Aryaman and Mitra ;
It is straightforward, Varuṇa, and thornless.
On that, O Ādityas, speak in our favour ;
Bestow on us invincible protection.

7. May Aryaman, may Aditi, kings' mother,
By easy paths through enmities transport us.
We would unscathed, possessed of many heroes,
Win Varuṇa's and Mitra's high protection.

8. Three earths, three heavens, too, these gods supported,
Three are their services within our synod.
By Law is mighty, Ādityas, your greatness
And fair, Aryaman, Varuṇa and Mitra.

9. Of golden aspect, radiant, bright, as sword-blades,
They have upheld the three light realms of heaven.
They slumber not, nor close their eyes, unfailing
They rule afar to help the truthful mortal.

10. Thou art, O Varuṇa, of all the sovereign,
Both of the gods, O Asura, and mortals.
To us vouchsafe to see a hundred autumns:
May we attain to lives prolonged and happy.

11. Neither the right nor left can I distinguish,
Neither before nor yet behind, Ādityas.
May I by you directed, reach with safety,
Bright gods, the light by innocence or wisdom.

12. Who to the kings that lead the law pays worship,
And whom thus constant blessings cause to flourish,
He, affluent, rides foremost in his chariot,
Bestowing gifts and in assemblies lauded.

13. He pure, unhurt by guile, with many heroes,
Robust, abides by waters rich in pasture.
Either from near or from afar none slay him
Who lives beneath the Ādityas' direction.

14. O Aditi and Varuṇa and Mitra,
Forgive us any sin we have committed.
May I obtain the light, secure and spacious,
O Indra; may long darkness never reach us.

15. Both worlds, combined, for him shed in abundance
The rain of heaven; fortunate and thriving
He goes to battle, both the mansions winning.
For him the world's two halves remain propitious.

16. Your wiles, intended, holy gods, for plotters,
Your nooses, Ādityas, for foes unloosened:
These would I pass, as with his car a driver;
May we unscathed be in your wide protection.

17. May I not ever lack a friendly patron,
Nor, Varuṇa, an open-handed comrade.
May I, O King, not want well-managed riches,
May we speak loud, with heroes, in the synod.

SŪRYA

Sūrya, who is addressed in about ten hymns of the *Rigveda*, is the most concrete of the solar deities, because his name designates the orb of the sun as well as the god. The solar disc is often called the eye of Sūrya, or the eye of Mitra-Varuṇa, as well as of Agni and of the gods. He is all-seeing, the spy of the whole world, beholding the good and bad deeds of mortals. His car is drawn by a single steed or by seven swift mares. The Dawn reveals or produces Sūrya; like a lover he follows the radiant goddess. He arouses men to activity; he is the soul of all that moves or stands. He is the son of Heaven (Dyaus). Sūrya is variously described as a bird traversing space; as a mottled bull or a brilliant steed; as a gem of the sky, or a variegated stone set in the midst of heaven; as a brilliant weapon; or as a wheel, though the wheel of Sūrya is also spoken of. He dispels the darkness, which he casts off like a skin. He measures the days and prolongs life. He drives away disease and evil dreams.

All creatures depend on him, and he is "all-creating." At his rising he is implored to declare men sinless to Mitra-Varuṇa and to other gods.

VI. SŪRYA

I, 115. METRE: TRIṢṬUBH.

1. The gods' refulgent countenance has risen,
   The eye of Mitra, Varuṇa and Agni.
   He has pervaded air, and earth, and heaven:
   The soul of all that moves and stands is Sūrya.

2. The Sun pursues the Dawn, the gleaming goddess,
   As a young man a maiden, to the region
   Where god-devoted men lay on the harness
   Of brilliant offerings for the brilliant godhead.

3. The brilliant steeds, bay coursers of the sun-god,
   Refulgent, dappled, meet for joyful praises,
   Wafting our worship, heaven's ridge have mounted,
   And in one day round earth and sky they travel.

4. This is the Sun's divinity, his greatness:
In midst of action he withdraws the daylight.
When from their stand he has withdrawn his coursers,
Then straightway night for him spreads out her garment.

5. This form the Sun takes in the lap of heaven,
That Varuṇa and Mitra may regard him.
One glow of his appears unending, splendid;
His bay steeds roll the other up, the black one.

6. To-day, O gods, do ye at Sūrya's rising
Release us from distress and from dishonour:
This boon may Varuṇa and Mitra grant us,
And Aditi and Sindhu, Earth and Heaven.

VII. SŪRYA

I, 50. METRE: 1-9 GĀYATRĪ; 10 ANUṢṬUBH.

1. Aloft his beams now bring the god
Who knows all creatures that are born,
That all may look upon the Sun.

2. Away like thieves the stars depart,
By the dark nights accompanied,
At the all-seeing Sun's approach.

3. His beams, his rays, have shone afar
Athwart the many homes of men,
Flaming aloft like blazing fires.

4. Swift-moving, visible to all,
Maker of light thou art, O Sun,
Illuming all the shining space.

5. Thou risest toward the host of gods
And toward the race of men: toward all,
That they may see the heavenly light.

7. The broad air traversing, the sky,
Thou metest, Sun, the days with nights,
Seeing all creatures that are born.

8. The seven bay mares that draw thy car,
Bring thee to us, far-seeing god,
O Sūrya of the gleaming hair.
9. The Sun has yoked the seven bright mares,
The shining daughters of his car :
With that self-yoking team he speeds.
10. Athwart the darkness gazing up,
To him the higher light, we now
Have soared to Sūrya, the god
Among the gods, the highest light.

PŪṢAN

This god, who is celebrated in eight hymns, has a vague personality, with few anthropomorphic traits. His foot, his right hand, his beard and his braided hair are mentioned. He carries a golden spear, an awl and a goad. His car is drawn by goats instead of horses. Gruel is his characteristic food. He sees all creatures clearly. He moves onward, observing the universe, and makes his abode in heaven. He is a guardian who knows and surveys all creatures. He traverses the distant path of heaven and earth. With his golden aerial ships he acts as the messenger of Sūrya. As best of charioteers he drove down the golden wheel of the sun. He is the wooer of his mother and the lover of his sister (*i.e.* Dawn), and was given by the gods as a husband to the Sun-maiden, Sūryā. One of his exclusive epithets is "glowing." He conducts the dead on the far-off path of the Fathers. A guardian of roads, he removes dangers out of the way. He protects cattle, bringing them home when lost. The meaning of the name is "Prosperer." The evidence thus indicates that Pūṣan was originally a solar deity, chiefly as a benevolent patron of pastoral prosperity.

VIII. PŪṢAN

I, 42. METRE : GĀYATRĪ.

1. O Pūṣan pass along the roads,
Free us, son of release, from care.
Guide us, going before, O god.

2. The wicked, ill-intentioned wolf,
Pūṣan, that lies in wait for us,
Him from our path smite thou away.

3. The robber lurking round our path,
Who there against us mischief plots,
Far from the track drive him away.

4. Tread under foot the burning brand
Of crafty and malignant men,
The miscreants whoe'er they be.

5. Pūṣan, that help of thine we claim,
O wonder-working, sapient god,
Wherewith our fathers thou didst aid.

6. Thou, lord of all prosperity,
Best wielder of the golden axe,
Make easy wealth for us to gain.

7. Past our pursuers lead us, make
Fair paths, easy for us to tread.
Thus, Pūṣan, show in us thy might.

8. Lead us to pastures rich in grass,
Send on the road no early heat.
Thus, Pūṣan, show in us thy might.

10. We wrangle not with Pūṣan, him
We call upon with songs of praise:
For wealth we seek the wondrous god.

SAVITAR

Savitar is invoked in eleven whole hymns and in a good many detached stanzas as well. He is pre-eminently a golden deity. His golden car is drawn by two or more brown, white-footed steeds. With his golden arms, which he raises aloft, he arouses and blesses all beings. His mighty golden splendour illumines heaven, earth and air. He moves in his golden car on an upward and a downward path, observing all creatures. Yellow-haired, he constantly raises his light in the east. On his ancient paths in the air he conveys the dead to where the righteous dwell. He drives away evil dreams and sins, demons and sorcerers. He observes fixed laws. Wind and waters are subject to, and regulated by him. He brings not only day but night, when he sends all beings to rest. The other gods follow his lead, and no being can resist his will. To Savitar is addressed the most famous stanza of the *Rigveda* (iii, 62, 10), which has been a morning prayer in India for more than 3,000 years. It is called the Sāvitrī, from the name of the god invoked, or Gāyatrī, from that of the metre in which it is composed :

> May we attain that excellent
> Glory of Savitar the God,
> That he may stimulate our thoughts.

Savitar is often distinguished from Sūrya, the sun. Thus he is said to shine with the rays of the sun, to impel the sun, or to declare men sinless to the sun. The name is derived from the root *sū*, "to stimulate," forms of which are perpetually used with it as an etymological play. The word *deva*, "god," is constantly associated with his name, as with that of no other deity, in the sense of the "stimulator god." Savitar is thus a solar deity in the capacity of the great stimulator of life and activity in the world.

IX. SAVITAR

VI, 71. METRE : 1-3 JAGATĪ ; 5-6 TRIṢṬUBH.

1. God Savitar, the dexterous, has stretched aloft
His arms, that he may stimulate all things to life.
Young, vigorous, most skilled, with fatness he
His hands besprinkles in the wide expanse of air.

2. May we possess god Savitar's most excellent
Impulsion, and enjoy his lavish gifts of wealth.
Thou art the god who sends to rest and wakes in turn
To life the whole two-footed and four-footed world.

3. With guards that never fail, auspicious, Savitar,
Protect our habitation all around to-day.
God of the golden tongue, for welfare ever new
Preserve us : let no plotter hold us in his grasp.

5. Like one who rouses, Savitar has stretched out
His golden arms that are so fair of aspect.
The heights of heaven and earth he has ascended,
And made each flying monster cease from troubling.

6. To-day wealth, Savitar, and wealth to-morrow,
Bring wealth to us each day by thine impulsion;
For over ample wealth, O god, thou rulest:
Through this our hymn may we of wealth be sharers.

VIṢṆU

Viṣṇu, though one of the two leading gods of modern Hinduism, is in the *Rigveda* as yet a minor deity, being addressed in only five or six hymns. The only anthropomorphic traits there attributed to him are that he is a youth of vast body and that he takes three strides. The latter is his chief characteristic, with which are associated his exclusive epithets of "wide-going" and "wide-striding." With these steps he traverses the earth and the terrestrial regions. Two of his steps are visible to men, but the third is beyond the flight of birds or mortal ken. His highest step is like an eye fixed in heaven; it shines down brightly. Viṣṇu's three strides undoubtedly refer to the course of the sun as it passes through the three divisions of the world: earth, air and heaven. Viṣṇu is further said to set in motion his 90 steeds (*i.e.* days) with their four names (*i.e.* seasons), in allusion to the 360 days of the solar year. Thus Viṣṇu seems to have been originally a personification of the sun in its activity of traversing the universe. Viṣṇu is described as taking his steps for man's existence, to bestow on him the earth as a dwelling place. The most prominent secondary characteristic of Viṣṇu is his friendship with Indra, with whom he is often allied in his conflict with Vṛtra. In hymns addressed to Viṣṇu alone, Indra is the only other god incidentally associated with him. One hymn invokes these two gods conjointly.

X. VIṢṆU

I, 154. METRE : TRIṢṬUBH.

1. I will proclaim the mighty deeds of Viṣṇu,
Of him who measured out the earthly spaces;
Who, firmly propping up the higher station,
Strode out in triple regions, widely pacing.

2. Because of this his mighty deed is Viṣṇu
Lauded, like some fierce beast that is much dreaded,
That wanders as it lists, that haunts the mountains:
He in whose three wide strides abide all creatures.

3. Let my inspiring hymn go forth to Viṣṇu,
The mountain-dwelling bull, the widely pacing,
Him who has measured out with but three footsteps,
Alone, this long and far-extended station;

4. Him whose three footsteps filled with mead, unfailing,
Revel in blissful joy; who has supported
Alone the universe in three divisions:
The earth and sky and all created beings.

5. I would attain to that his dear dominion
Where men devoted to the gods do revel.
In the wide-striding Viṣṇu's highest footstep
There is a spring of mead: such is our kinship.

6. We long to go to those your dwelling-places
Where are the kine with many horns, the nimble:
For thence, indeed, the highest step of Viṣṇu,
Wide-pacing bull, shines brightly down upon us.

USHAS

Uṣas, the goddess of Dawn, who is celebrated in some twenty hymns of the *Rigveda*, is but slightly personified, for the underlying physical phenomenon is never absent from the mind of the poet. She appears in the east, clothed in light, adorned with bright raiment like a dancer. She drives away the darkness and removes the black robe of night. Though ancient, she is ever young, being born again and again. She wastes away the life of mortals. She opens the gates of heaven, and her radiant beams appear like herds of cattle. She rides on a brilliant car, drawn by ruddy steeds or kine. She drives away bad dreams, evil spirits and the hateful darkness. When she shines forth, the birds fly from their nests, and men seek nourishment. She appears day after day at the appointed place, never infringing the law of nature and of the gods. She is born in the sky, and is constantly called the "daughter of heaven." She is also the elder sister of night (p. 41), with whose name hers is often joined as a compound in the dual. She is closely associated with the Sun, who is her lover, following her as a young man a maiden. She thus often becomes the wife of Sūrya. But as preceding the sun, she is sometimes called his mother, and is thus said to arrive with a bright child. The sacrificial fire being lit at dawn, Uṣas is often associated with Agni, whom she causes to be kindled and who is sometimes called her lover. She is also often connected with the Aśvins, the twin gods of early morning. As disclosing the treasures concealed by darkness, she distributes them liberally and is characteristically "bountiful." She not only brings the worshipper wealth and children, but bestows protection and long life, fame and glory on the benefactors of the poet.

Forms of the root *vas*, "to shine," from which the name of Uṣas is derived, are often used in describing her activity, somewhat in the same way as *sū*, "to stimulate," is used with the name of Savitar (p. 33).

XI. UṢAS

I, 92. METRE: 4 JAGATĪ; 5-12 TRIṢṬUBH; 13-15 UṢṆIH.

4. She throws gay garments round her like a dancing girl;
E'en as a cow her udder, she displays her breast.
Creating light for all the world, Dawn has unbarred
The gates of darkness as when cows break from their stall.

5. Her radiant shimmer has appeared before us ;
It spreads, and drives away the swarthy monster.
As one anoints the post at sacrifices
The daughter of the sky extends her lustre.

6. We have crossed to the farther shore of darkness:
Dawn shining forth, her webs of light is weaving.
She smiles for glory, radiant, like a lover.
To show good will she, fair of face, has wakened.

7. The radiant leader of rich gifts, the daughter
Of Heaven by the Gotamas is lauded.
Mete out to us, O Dawn, largesses: offspring,
Brave men, conspicuous wealth in cows and horses.

8. May I attain that wealth renowned and ample,
With many heroes, troops of friends, and horses,
O Dawn, that shinest forth with wondrous glory,
Urged on by mighty strength, auspicious lady.

9. Looking on all created things, the goddess
Shines far and wide, facing the eye of Sūrya.
Awaking every living soul to motion,
She has aroused the voice of every thinker.

10. Born newly again and again though ancient,
Herself adorning with the selfsame colour,
The goddess wears away the life of mortals,
Like stakes diminished by a skilful gambler.

11. The ends of heaven disclosing, she awakens;
To distance far she banishes her sister.
Diminishing the years of life, the maiden
Flushes afar with the light of her lover.

12. Gracious and bright, spreading her rays like cattle,
As a river its flood, afar she glimmers.
Infringing not the gods' unchanging statutes,
She flushes radiant with the beams of Sūrya.

13. O Dawn, bring us that brilliant wealth,
O thou that bearest rich rewards,
Whereby both sons and grandsons we may well maintain.

14. Refulgent Dawn, to-day and here,
Thou that art rich in kine and steeds,
Shine forth on us abundant wealth, goddess benign.

15. Yoke, Dawn, to-day thy ruddy steeds,
O thou that bearest rich rewards:
Then on thy car to us all fortune's gifts convey.

XII. UṢAS

I, 113. METRE : TRIṢṬUBH.

1. This light has come, of all the lights the fairest:
The brilliant brightness has been born effulgent.
Urged onward for god Savitar's uprising,
Night now has yielded up her place to morning.

2. Bringing a radiant calf she comes resplendent:
To her the Black one has given up her mansions.
Akin, immortal, following each the other,
Morning and Night fare on, exchanging colours.

3. The sisters' pathway is the same, unending:
Taught by the gods alternately they tread it.
Fair-shaped, of form diverse, yet single-minded,
Morning and Night clash not, nor do they tarry.

4. Bright leader of glad sounds she shines effulgent:
Widely she has unclosed for us her portals.
Pervading all the world she shows us riches:
Dawn has awakened every living creature.

5. Men lying on the ground she wakes to action:
Some rise to seek enjoyment of great riches,
Some, seeing little, to behold the distant:
Dawn has awakened every living creature.

6. One for dominion, and for fame another;
Another is aroused for winning greatness;
Another seeks the goal of varied nurture:
Dawn has awakened every living creature.

7. Daughter of Heaven, she has appeared before us,
A maiden shining in resplendent raiment.
Thou sovereign lady of all earthly treasure,
Auspicious Dawn, shine here to-day upon us.

8. The path of those that have gone by she follows,
The first of endless dawns to come hereafter.
The living at her rising she arouses;
The dead she never wakens from their slumber.

9. O Dawn, since thou hast made them kindle Agni,
Since thou hast shone forth with the light of Sūrya,
Since thou the sacrificer hast awakened:
Thou hast performed among the gods good service.

10. How distant is the time when she comes midway
Between the past and those to shine in future?
The earlier dawns right willingly she follows.
Expected, she fulfils the later's wishes.

11. Gone are those mortals who in former ages
Beheld the flushing of the early morning;
We living men now look upon her shining:
Those will be born who shall hereafter see her.

12. Dispelling foes, observer of world order,
Born in due season, giver of enjoyment,
Wafting oblations, bringing wealth and fortune,
Shine brightly here to-day, O Dawn, upon us.

13. The goddess Dawn has flushed in former ages,
And here to-day the bounteous maiden flushes:
So also may she flush in days hereafter.
With powers her own she fares, immortal, ageless.

14. In the sky's framework she has gleamed with brightness;
The goddess has cast off the robe of darkness.
Rousing the world from sleep, with ruddy horses,
Dawn in her well-yoked chariot is arriving.

15. She brings upon it many bounteous blessings;
Brightly she shines and spreads her brilliant lustre.
Last of innumerable morns departed,
First of bright morns to come, has Dawn arisen.

16. Arise! The vital breath again has reached us:
Darkness has gone away and light is coming.
She leaves a pathway for the sun to travel:
We have arrived where men prolong existence.

17. The singer lauding the refulgent mornings,
Like charioteer with reins, sends forth his message:
To-day this grant thy praiser, bounteous goddess:
Life rich in offspring shine thou down upon us.

18. The dawns that shine forth for the pious mortal,
Bestowing kine and steeds and many heroes:
May these be gained by zealous Soma-pressers,
When joyous songs break forth like gusty breezes.

19. Mother of gods and Aditi's effulgence,
Banner of sacrifice, shine forth exalted.
Shine forth and look upon our prayer with favour:
Bounteous, cause fruitfulness among the people.

20. What brilliant wealth the dawns convey, auspicious,
To bless the zealous offerer of worship,
All that may Varuṇa and Mitra grant us,
And Aditi and Sindhu, Earth and Heaven.

RĀTRĪ

The following is the only hymn of the *Rigveda* in which, under the name of Rātrī, the goddess of night is invoked. Like her sister, Uṣas, she is a daughter of Heaven. She is conceived not as the dark, but as the bright, starlit night, shining with her eyes. Decked with all splendour, she drives away the darkness. At her approach, men, beasts and birds go to rest. Protecting her worshippers from the wolf and the thief, she guides them to safety. Under the name of *nakta* combined with *uṣas*, Night appears as a dual divinity with Dawn in some twenty scattered stanzas of the *Rigveda*.

XIII. NIGHT

X, 127. METRE: GĀYATRĪ.

1. When night comes on, the goddess shines
In many places with her eyes:
All glorious she has decked herself.

2. Immortal goddess far and wide,
She fills the valleys and the heights:
Darkness she drives away with light.

3. The goddess now, as she comes on,
Is turning out her sister, Dawn:
Far off the darkness hastes away.

4. So, goddess, come to-day to us:
At thy approach we seek our homes,
As birds their nests upon the tree.

5. The villagers have gone to rest
And footed beasts and wingèd birds;
The hungry hawk himself is still.

6. Ward off from us she-wolf and wolf,
Ward off the robber, goddess Night:
So take us safe across the gloom.

7. The darkness, thickly painting black,
Has, palpable, come nigh to me:
Like debts, O Dawn, clear it away.

8. I have brought up a hymn, like kine,
For thee, as one who wins a fight:
This, Heaven's daughter, Night, accept.

THE AŚVINS

Next to Indra, Agni and Soma, the twin deities, called Aśvins, "Horsemen," are the most prominent gods in the *Rigveda*, being invoked in more than 50 entire hymns and in parts of several others. The time of their appearance is between dawn and sunrise, when darkness still abides among the ruddy cows (*i.e.* the rays of dawn). Uṣas awakens them; she is followed by them on their car. They dispel darkness and drive away evil spirits. Their car, which was fashioned by the three divine artificers, the Ṛbhus, and is sunlike and golden, is threefold and has three wheels. It is drawn by horses, or by birds, or by winged steeds. Its revolving course traverses heaven and earth in one day.

The Aśvins are the children of Heaven, but are once called the sons of Vivasvant (the sun) and Saraṇyū (probably the dawn). Pūṣan is once said to be their son, and Dawn is probably meant by their sister. They are often associated with the daughter of the sun, Sūryā, who rides with them on their car and is their spouse.

The Aśvins are twins and inseparable. They are young and yet ancient, handsome, lords of lustre, of golden brightness, adorned with lotus garlands, and they follow a golden path. They are more closely associated than any of the other gods with mead (*madhu*), which they desire and drink. But they are also fond of Soma, which they drink with Uṣas and Sūrya. They possess profound wisdom and occult power, but their two most frequent epithets are "wondrous" and "true." Typically rescuers from distress, they are divine physicians, who cure diseases with their remedies, healing the sick and maimed, and restoring youth and sight. Many legends are told of those whom they befriended, especially that of Bhujyu, whom they saved in a ship from the ocean. The meaning of their name is "the two horsemen," not, however, as riders, but as charioteers. They evidently belong to the group of the deities of light, but the actual phenomenon which they represent is doubtful. The two most probable theories are that they originally represented either the morning twilight, as half light and half dark, or the morning and evening star. They probably go back to the Indo-European period, being akin to the two famous horsemen of Greek mythology, the sons of Zeus, brothers of Helena; and to the two Lettic god's sons, who come riding on their steeds to woo the daughter of the sun.

XIV. THE AŚVINS

VIII, 71. METRE: TRIṢṬUBH.

1. Night hastens far away from Dawn, her sister;
   The Black one yields the ruddy god a pathway.
   We call on you two rich in kine and horses:
   By day and night ward off from us the arrow.

2. Come to the pious mortal bringing bounty,
   O Aśvins, hither with your chariot speeding.

Do ye ward off from us disease and weakness.
By day and night, lovers of sweetness, guard us.

3. May your propitious coursers whirl your chariot
Toward us at the dawn now flushing on us.
Bring it, by traces drawn and fraught with riches,
Hither with horses yoked by Order, Aśvins.

4. That car, three-seated, lords of men, that bears you
With riches laden well, drives forth at daybreak:
On it, O Nāsatyas, to us come onward,
That, with all nurture fraught, it may approach us.

5. Once from old age ye two released Chyavāna;
With a swift courser ye presented Pedu;
Ye rescued Atri from distress and darkness;
The fettered Jāhusha ye placed in freedom.

6. To you this thought, this song is offered, Aśvins,
This hymn of praise enjoy, ye mighty heroes.
From us these prayers have gone, to you directed.
Ye gods protect us evermore with blessings.

INDRA

Indra, being the favourite national god of the Vedic people, is invoked in about one-fourth of the hymns of the *Rigveda*—in far more than are addressed to any other deity. He is more anthropomorphic and more invested with mythological imagery than any other Vedic god. He is primarily a deity of the thunderstorm, who vanquishes the demons of drought or darkness, setting free the waters or winning the light. His physical parts, such as his body and his head, are often mentioned. His form, as well as his hair and his beard, is tawny. His two arms are specially often referred to as wielding the thunderbolt (*vajra*), which is his exclusive weapon. This missile, fashioned for him by the artificer god, Tvaṣṭar, is made of iron, but sometimes of stone, is sharp and many-pointed, and golden or tawny in colour. Sometimes he is armed with bow and arrows, and he also carries a hook. His golden car is drawn by two tawny steeds.

Indra is, more than any other god, addicted to Soma, which stimulates him to carry out his warlike deeds, especially the slaughter of the demon Vṛtra. One entire hymn consists of a monologue in which Indra, intoxicated with Soma, boasts of his greatness and his might. The inference from some hymns is that his father is Dyaus (Heaven), but from others that he is Tvaṣṭar. Agni and Pūṣan are his brothers. His wife, often mentioned, is Indrāṇī. He is associated with various other deities. The Maruts, or storm gods, are his chief allies in conflicts. Agni is the god most often conjoined with him as a dual divinity. He is often also coupled with Varuṇa and Vāyu, less often with Soma, Bṛhaspati, Pūṣan and Viṣṇu.

Indra is described as vast in size. His greatness and power are constantly dwelt on and emphasized by various epithets applied to him exclusively.

The essential myth that forms the basis of his nature is described with great frequency and much variation. Exhilarated by Soma and generally accompanied by the Maruts, Indra attacks the chief demon of drought, usually called Vṛtra, but also often the serpent. Heaven and earth tremble when the mighty combat takes place. With his bolt he shatters Vṛtra, who encompasses the waters. The result of the conflict, which is regarded as being constantly renewed, is that Indra pierces the mountain and sets free the waters pent up like imprisoned cows. The physical elements in the conflict are nearly always the bolt, mountains, waters or rivers, while lightning, thunder, cloud, rain are seldom directly named. The waters are often terrestrial, but also aerial and celestial. The clouds are the mountains on which the demons lie or dwell, or from which he casts them down, or which he cleaves to release the waters. Or the cloud is a rock which encompasses the cows (as the waters are sometimes called), and from which he sets them free. Clouds, as holding the waters, figure as cows also; they appear, moreover, under the names of udder, spring, cask, or pail. The clouds further figure as the fortresses of the aerial demons, being described as moving, autumnal, made of iron or stone, and as ninety, ninety-nine, or a hundred in number. Indra, who shatters them, is therefore called the "fort-destroyer." But his chief and specific epithet is "Vṛtra-slayer," as expressing his main activity. In his fight with the demon the Maruts are his regular allies, though Agni, Soma, and Viṣṇu also often assist him. Indra also fights with various minor demons; sometimes he destroys demons in general (Rakṣases or Asuras).

With the release of the waters is connected the winning of light, sun and dawn. Thus Indra is invoked to slay Vṛtra and to win the light. When he had slain Vṛtra and released the waters for man, he placed the sun visibly in the heavens. The sun shone forth when Indra blew the serpent from the air. In this connexion there is often no mention of the Vṛtra fight. Indra is then simply said to find the light; he gained the sun or found it in the darkness, making a path for it. He produces the dawn as well as the sun; he opens the darkness with the dawn and the sun. The cows mentioned along with the sun and dawn, or with the sun alone, as found or won by Indra, are here probably the morning beams, which are elsewhere compared with cattle coming out of their dark stalls. Thus when the dawns went to meet Indra, he became the lord of the cows; when he overcame Vṛtra, he made visible the cows of the nights. There seems to be a confusion between the restoration of the sun after the darkness of the thunderstorm and the recovery of the sun from the darkness of night at dawn. The latter feature is probably an extension of the former. With the Vṛtra fight and the winning of the cows and of the sun, is also connected the gaining of Soma. Thus when Indra drove the serpent from the air, there shone forth fires, the sun, and the Soma; he won Soma at the same time as the cows.

Great cosmic actions are often ascribed to Indra: he settled the quaking mountains and plains; he stretches out heaven and earth like a hide; he holds asunder heaven and earth; he turned the non-existent into the existent in a moment.

As the destroyer of demons in combat, Indra is constantly invoked by warriors. As the great god of battle he is more frequently called upon than any other deity to help the Aryans in their conflicts with earthly enemies. He protects the Aryan colour and subjects the black skin. He dispersed 50,000 of the black race. He subjected the Dasyus to the Aryan, on whom he bestowed land.

More generally, Indra is the protector, helper and friend of his worshippers. He grants them wealth, regarded as the result of victories. His liberality is so characteristic that the epithet "Bountiful" (*maghavan*) is almost exclusively restricted to him.

Several minor myths are connected with Indra. One of them is that of the winning of Soma: it is to him that the eagle brings the draught of immortality from the highest heaven. Another is the capture by Indra, with the help of Saramā, of the cows confined in a cave by demons called Paṇis.

Moreover, various stories containing mythological elements, but probably having a historical foundation, are told about Indra's fighting in aid of individual men, such as king Sudās, against terrestrial foes.

Indra forms a striking contrast to Varuṇa, the other divine universal monarch of the *Rigveda*. His attributes are mainly those of physical superiority, and rule over the physical world. He is violent in action, an irresistible warrior, a lavisher of spoils on mankind, but also sensual and immoral in various ways, such as excess in eating and drinking, and cruelty in killing his father, Tvaṣṭar. Varuṇa, on the other hand, wields passive and peaceful sway, applies the laws of nature with uniformity, upholds moral order, and in his character displays lofty ethical features.

Indra is pre-Vedic, for his name occurs in the *Avesta* as that of demon; and the term Vṛtra-slayer, as a designation of the god of Victory, occurs there, though unconnected with Indra. It is therefore probable

Then ye two smote the Dāsa and the Aryan foes:
Ye favoured, Indra-Varuṇa, Sudās with help.

2. Where men with banners raised in fight together rush,
In battle conflict where there is no pleasant thing,
Where creatures fear the god who sees the heavenly light,
O Indra-Varuṇa, be there our advocates.

3. Earth's ends appear enwrapt in dust, O Varuṇa
And Indra; now the din has mounted to the sky;
The onset of the warriors rolls close up to me:
Come hither with your aid, O ye that hear my call.

4. O Varuṇa and Indra, Bheda ye attacked
With weapons irresistibly, and helped Sudās.
Ye heard his fighters' prayers when they called to you:
Then was the Tṛtsus' priestly service justified.

5. My foes' malignities, O Indra-Varuṇa,
My enemies' assaults press me on every side.
Since ye control the property of friend and foe,
Do ye then favour us on war's decisive day.

6. Both sides in battle-conflicts call upon you two,
O Indra-Varuṇa, intent on gaining wealth,
Where once ye helped Sudās with all his Tṛtsu host,
When by the ten kings' hostile force hard pressed in fight.

7. Ten kings allied, who worshipped not, did not prevail
Against Sudās in war, O Indra-Varuṇa;
The lauds of heroes sitting at the feast came true:
The gods were at their invocations on their side.

8. Ye gave Sudās hemmed in on every side your aid,
When ten kings fought against him, Indra-Varuṇa,
Where filled with thought the Tṛtsus, wearing braided hair
And clad in white, with homage and devotion prayed.

9. The one in battle-conflicts slays the demon foes,
The other evermore his sacred statutes guards.
We call on you with well-turned hymns, O mighty ones:
To us, O Indra-Varuṇa, protection grant.

10. May Indra, Mitra, Varuṇa and Aryaman,
To us fair fame and great, far-reaching shelter grant.
We think of the unfailing light of Aditi,
Who loves the law, and of the call of Savitar.

PARJANYA

Parjanya is a subordinate deity in the *Rigveda*, being invoked in three hymns only. He is a rain-god. The name often means "rain-cloud," but generally represents its personification. It is often alluded to as an udder, a pail, or a water-skin. Parjanya is frequently spoken of as a bull that quickens the plants and the earth. The shedding of rain is his most prominent characteristic: he flies around with a watery car and loosens the water-skin, shedding rain-water as our divine father; he is then associated with thunder and lightning. He is in a special degree a nourisher of vegetation, and also a producer of animal fertility. He is several times called a father. He is once said to be the son of heaven, and his wife is by implication the earth.

XVIII. PARJANYA

V, 83. METRE: 1.5-8, 10 TRIṢṬUBH; 2-4 JAGATĪ; 9 ANUṢṬUBH.

1. Invoke the mighty god with songs of welcome;
Parjanya praise: with homage seek to win him.
He, roaring like a bull, with streams that quicken,
A seed to germinate in plants deposits.

2. The trees he shatters and he smites the demon host:
The whole world trembles at his mighty weapon's stroke,
The guiltless man himself flees from the potent god,
When miscreants Parjanya with his thunder strikes.

3. Like charioteer his horses lashing with a whip,
The god makes manifest his messengers of rain.
From far away the roaring of the lion sounds,
What time Parjanya veils the firmament with rain.

4. The winds blow forth; to earth the quivering lightnings fall,
The plants shoot up; with moisture streams the realm of light.
For all the world abundant nourishment is born,
When by Parjanya Earth is fertilized with seed.

5. O thou at whose behest the earth bows downward,
O thou at whose behest hoofed creatures quiver,
At whose behest by plants all shapes are taken:
As such, Parjanya, grant to us strong shelter.

6. The rain of heaven bestow, O Maruts, on us,
Of your strong steed pour forth the streams abundant.
With this thy thundering roar do thou come hither,
And shed the waters as our heavenly father.

7. With roar and thunder now the germ deposit,
Fly round us with thy water-bearing chariot.
Turn well thy water-skin unloosened downward,
Make, with the waters, heights and hollows level.

8. Draw the great bucket up and pour it downward,
And let the liberated streams flow forward.
On all sides drench both heaven and earth with fatness;
Let there be for the cows fair pools for drinking.

9. When, O Parjanya, roaring loud,
Thou slay'st with thunder wicked men,
This universe rejoices then,
And everything that is on earth.

10. Thou hast shed rain; pray now withhold it wholly;
Thou hast made passable all desert places.
To serve as food thou hast made plants to flourish:
And hast received the gratitude of creatures.

RUDRA

Rudra is invoked alone in only three entire hymns. His hand, his arms, and his limbs are mentioned, and he is described as having beautiful lips and braided hair. He is brown in colour and shines like the radiant sun, being arrayed in golden ornaments and wearing a glorious necklace. He drives in a car; he holds the thunderbolt in his arm, and discharges his lightning shaft from the sky; but he is usually armed with a bow and arrows.

Rudra is often associated with the Maruts, whose father he is. He is fierce and destructive like a terrible beast, being called a bull and the ruddy boar of heaven. He is unsurpassed in might, young and unaging, a lord and father of the world. By his rule and universal dominion he is aware of the doings of men and gods. He is bountiful, easily invoked and auspicious. But he is usually malevolent; for the hymns addressed to him chiefly express fear of his terrible shafts and deprecation of his wrath. He is implored not to slay or injure, in his anger, his worshippers and their belongings, but to avert his great malignity and his cow-slaying, man-slaying bolt from them. But he is not purely maleficent like a demon. He not only preserves from calamity, but bestows blessings. His healing powers are often mentioned. He has a thousand remedies and is the greatest of physicians. The phenomenon underlying Rudra's nature is not quite clear; but it was probably the storm, not pure and simple, but in its baleful aspect as manifested in the destructive agency of lightning. His healing and beneficent powers would then have been founded partly on the fertilizing and purifying action of the thunderstorm, and partly on the negative action of sparing those whom he might slay. Thus the deprecations of his wrath led to the application to him of the euphemistic epithet, *Śiva*, "Auspicious," the regular name of Rudra's historical successor in post-Vedic mythology.

XIX. RUDRA

II, 33. METRE : TRIṢṬUBH

1. Let thy goodwill, O father of the Maruts,
Light on us : part us not from Sūrya's vision.
In mercy may the hero spare our horses :
May we, O Rudra, have abundant offspring.

2. By thy most wholesome remedies, O Rudra,
Thy gifts, I would attain a hundred autumns.
Drive far away from us distress and hatred,
Drive far away, wide-scattered, all diseases.

3. Of what is born thou art the chief in glory,
Armed with the thunder, mightiest of the mighty.
Transport us to the farther shore of trouble
In safety ; frustrate all attacks of mischief.

4. May we not anger thee with homage, Rudra,
Nor with ill-praises, nor joint invocation.
Raise up, O Bull, with remedies our heroes :
I hear of thee as best of all physicians.

5. With invocations and oblations summoned
Rudra I would appease with my laudations :
May he, soft-hearted, easily appealed to,
Brown-hued, fair-lipped, not to his wrath subject us.

6. The bull, escorted by the Maruts, gladdens
Me who invokes, with his most forceful vigour.
I, sound, would reach, as in the heat, a shelter :
Rudra's good will I would desire to capture.

7. Where is that gracious hand of thine, O Rudra,
That is so full of remedies and coolness ?
As the remover of all god-sent damage,
Do thou, O Bull, now show compassion towards me.

8. Forth for the brown and whitish bull I utter
A mighty panegyric of the mighty.
I will adore the radiant god with homage.
We praise the terrifying name of Rudra.

9. He, mighty, brown-hued, multiform, has decked out
His stalwart limbs with jewels bright and golden,

From Rudra, this great universe's ruler,
Let not be severed his divine dominion.

10. Worthy, thou carriest thy bow and arrows,
Worthy, thine honourèd and all-hued necklace
Worthy, thou wieldest all this mighty power.
Naught that exists is mightier than thou art.

11. Praise him the famed, who sits upon the car-seat
The young, the fierce, like a dread beast, a slayer.
When praised, be gracious, Rudra, to the singer:
Let thy darts pass us and lay low another.

12. I bow down like a son before his father,
Who with good will comes nigh to him, O Rudra.
I praise the true lord, of much wealth the giver:
To us thou grantest remedies when lauded.

13. Those remedies of yours, the pure, O Maruts,
That are most wholesome, mighty ones, and potent,
That Manu chose in ancient days, our Father:
Those I desire, and Rudra's balm and blessing.

14. May Rudra's missile turn aside and pass us,
May the fierce Rudra's great ill-will go by us.
Relax thy rigid bow to save our patrons;
Spare, O thou god of bounty, child and grandchild.

15. So brown-hued, mighty Rudra, widely famous,
Here to our invocations be attentive,
As not, O god, to rise in wrath and slay us.
May we speak loud with heroes in the synod.

MARUTS

The Maruts, or Storm-gods, are prominent deities in the *Rigveda*, being invoked in 33 hymns alone, and in 9 others in association with other gods (Indra, Agni, Pūṣan). They form a group, being mentioned in the plural only. Their number is stated as thrice seven or thrice sixty. They are the sons of Rudra and Pṛśni (who probably represents the mottled storm-cloud). But they are also said to have been generated by Vāyu, god of wind, or to be the sons of heaven, or even to be self-born. They are brothers of equal age, having the same birthplace and abode. The goddess Rodasī is always connected with them as riding on their car. She seems to have been regarded as their bride.

The brilliance of the Maruts is characteristic, and they are very frequently associated with lightning. They have spears of lightning and wear golden helmets. They are armed with golden axes, but sometimes with bows and arrows, like their father Rudra. They wear golden mantles, and golden ornaments, garlands, armlets and anklets. Their cars gleam with lightning, being drawn by steeds (generally feminine) that are ruddy, tawny, or spotted.

The noise made by the Maruts, often mentioned, is thunder and the roaring of the winds. They cause the mountains to quake and the two worlds to tremble; they shatter trees and, like wild elephants, devour the forests. They are often called singers: they sing a song; they are the singers of heaven; for Indra, when he slew the dragon, they sang a song and pressed Soma. Their song, though primarily representing the sound of the winds, is also conceived as a hymn of praise. Thus they come to be compared with priests and are even addressed as such.

One of the main activities of the Maruts is to shed rain: they cover the eye of the sun with rain; they create darkness with the cloud when they shed rain; they cause the celestial pail and the streams of the mountains to pour. The waters shed by them are often clearly connected with the thunderstorm. Their rain is often figuratively called milk, ghee, or honey. They avert heat, but also dispel darkness, produce light, and prepare a path for the sun.

More generally the Maruts are described as young and unaging, dustless, mighty, fierce, terrible like lions, but also playful like children or calves.

Owing to their connexion with the thunderstorm, the Maruts are constantly associated with Indra as his friends and allies, who increase his strength and his prowess with their songs, prayers, and hymns, and generally assist him in his fight with Vṛtra. Indra, in fact, accomplishes all his celestial feats in their company. But sometimes the Maruts accomplish these same feats alone.

When they are not associated with Indra, the Maruts occasionally exhibit the maleficent traits of their father Rudra. Hence they are implored to ward off their lightning from their worshippers and not to let their ill-will reach them, and are besought to avert their arrow and the stone which they hurl, their lightning, and their cow- and man-slaying bolt. But, like their father Rudra, they are also supplicated to bring healing remedies. These remedies appear to be the waters, for the Maruts bestow medicine by raining.

The evidence of the *Rigveda* shows that the Maruts are storm-gods. Etymologically the word may mean either the "Shiners" or the "Crushers."

XX. MARUTS

VIII, 7. METRE: GĀYATRĪ.

1. When, Maruts, now for you the sage
Pours out the threefold Soma draught,
Ye shine forth on the mountain heights.

2. Whenever, bright ones, growing strong,
You have decided on your course,
The mountains bend and bow themselves.

3. Loud roaring with the winds, the sons
Of Pṛśni raise themselves aloft:
They have milked out the swelling draught.

4. The Maruts scatter mist abroad,
They make the mountain ridges quake,
When with the winds they go their way.

5. When mountains bow before your march,
And rivers, too, before your rule,
Before your mighty, roaring blast:

6. On you we call by night for aid
On you we call aloud by day,
On you while sacrifice proceeds.

7. They rise, of ruddy hue and bright,
Upon their courses with a roar,
Across the ridges of the sky.

8. With power they shoot a ray of light
So that the sun may run his course;
They with their beams spread far and wide.

9. Accept, O Maruts, this my song,
Ṛbhukṣans, this my hymn of praise,
Accept ye now this call of mine.

10. The dappled cows have milked three lakes,
Mead for the wielder of the bolt,
Out of the spring, the water-cask.

11. O Maruts, pray come here to us,
Whenever, seeking your good will,
We call you hither from the sky.

12. For, Rudras and Ṛbhukṣans, ye,
O bounteous ones, are in our house
And wise when ye enjoy the draught.

13. From heaven, Maruts, bring to us
Abundant wealth distilling joy,
With plenteous food all-nourishing.

14. When you, as if from mountain tops,
Have, bright ones, willed to take your way,
You in the drops distilled rejoice.

15. The mortal with his prayers should ask
The favour and goodwill of that
Great host of theirs invincible.

16. They who, like sparks, with showers of rain,
Blow onward through both heaven and earth,
And milk the spring that never fails:

17. The sons of Pṛśni rise aloft,
With chariots and with rattling sounds,
With rushing winds and songs of praise.

18. For riches, let us surely win
Your help that aided Turvaśa,
Yadu, Kaṇva, who gained great wealth.

19. Like butter swelling, may these draughts,
Accompanied by Kāṇva's hymns,
Increase your strength, ye bounteous ones.

20. Where, bounteous Maruts, do ye now
Rejoice, for whom the straw is spread,
What Brahman priest is serving you?

21. For ye, for whom the straw is spread,
Do not, as once ye did for praise,
Rejoice our sacrificers' ranks.

22. Together they have brought both worlds,
The mighty waters, and the sun,
And, joint by joint, the thunderbolt.

23. They joint by joint have Vṛtra rent,
And rent the gloomy mountain clouds,
Performing an heroic feat.

24. They reinforced the mighty strength
And skill of Trita as he fought,
And Indra in the Vṛtra-fray.

25. Celestial, lightnings in their hands,
They wear gold helmets on their heads;
For glory, bright, they deck themselves.

26. When eagerly from far ye came
Nigh to the cavern of the bull,
With fear, like Heaven, he roared aloud.

27. Brought by your golden-footed steeds
Come hither, O ye gods, to us,
To take from us our sacrifice.

28. When the red leader in their car
The spotted deer directs, the bright
Gods go: may they the waters free.

30. When will ye with your favours come,
O Maruts, hither to the sage,
The suppliant who calls you thus?

31. How is it now? Who are your friends,
Since ye left Indra in the lurch?
Who in your friendship counts to-day?

32. I praise, O Kaṇvas, Agni with
The Maruts holding in their hands
The bolt and wearing swords of gold.

33. I would draw sure for welfare new
The mighty gods adorable
All hither with their splendid spoil.

34. The very hills before them sink,
Deeming themselves but side-ravines ;
The very mountains bow down low.

35. Their steeds that have a transverse course,
Convey them flying through the air,
To him that lauds them giving strength.

36. The ancient Agni has been born
With brilliance like the shining sun ;
They with their beams spread far and wide.

VĀTA

The god of Wind is invoked by the two names of Vāyu and Vāta, both derived from the root *vā*, "to blow." The former is addressed in one whole hymn and parts of others, the latter in two short hymns. Both names are sometimes used in the same verse, but Vāyu is more often the god, Vāta the element. In keeping with the latter distinction, Vāyu is often associated with the anthropomorphic Indra as a dual divinity, while Vāta is similarly coupled with Parjanya, whose connexion with the thunderstorm is more vivid and realistic than that of Indra. Different sets of epithets are applied to these two wind-gods. Vāyu has a shining car drawn by a team or by a pair of ruddy steeds. He is fond of Soma, and is its protector. He grants fame, offspring and wealth; he disperses foes and protects the weak. Vāta is the breath of the gods; like Rudra he wafts healing and prolongs life, for he has the treasure of immortality in his house. He is chiefly mentioned in connexion with the thunderstorm, and his noise is often referred to. He produces ruddy lights and makes the dawns to shine. His swiftness often supplies a comparison for the speed of the gods or of mythical steeds.

XXI. VĀTA

X, 168. METRE: TRIṢṬUBH.

1. Of Vāta's car I now will praise the greatness:
Rending it speeds along; its noise is thunder.
Touching the sky it flies, creating lightnings;
Scattering dust it traverses earth's ridges.

2. The hosts of Vāta onward speed together:
They haste to him as women to a concourse.
The god with them upon the same car mounted,
The king of all this universe speeds onward.

3. In air, along his pathways speeding onward,
Never on any day he tarries resting.
The first-born order-loving friend of waters:
Where was he born, and whence has he arisen?

4. Of gods the breath, and of the world the offspring,
This god according to his liking wanders.
His sound is heard, his form is never looked on:
That Vāta let us worship with oblation.

ĀPAS: WATERS

The waters, which are invoked in four entire hymns, as well as in a few detached stanzas, are personified only to the extent of being thought of as mothers, young wives and goddesses, bestowing boons and coming to the sacrifice. They follow the path of the gods. They flow in a channel dug out with his bolt by Indra, whose ordinances they never infringe. The sea is their goal. But they are also celestial; for their abode is with the gods, in the seat of Mitra-Varuṇa, beside the sun. King Varuṇa moves in their midst, looking down on the truth and falsehood of men. As mothers they produce not only Agni (p. 73), but all that is fixed or moves. They purify and carry away defilement. They also cleanse from moral guilt—from the sins of violence, cursing and lying. They further bestow remedies, health, strength, long life, wealth and immortality. Their favour is often invoked, and they are invited to receive the Soma libation, seated on the sacrificial grass.

The waters are often associated with honey: their milk mixed with honey is produced in the sky, gladdens the gods, and became the drink of Indra (p. 43), giving him heroic strength. Here the celestial waters seem to be identified with the heavenly Soma. Elsewhere the waters used in preparing the terrestrial Soma seem to be meant. Thus they appear, bearing ghee and honey, in accord with the priests that bring well-pressed Soma for Indra. Soma delights in them as a young man in lovely maidens. He approaches them as a lover; before him, the youth, they, the maidens, bow down.

The deification of the waters is pre-Vedic, for they are invoked in the *Avesta* also.

XXII. WATERS

VII, 49. METRE: TRIṢṬUBH.

1. With ocean for their chief they flow unresting;
From the aërial flood they hasten cleansing;
For whom the mighty Indra's bolt cut channels,
Here may those waters, goddesses, preserve me.

2. Waters that come from heaven or run in channels
Dug out, or flow spontaneously by nature,
That, clear and pure, have as their goal the ocean:
Here may those waters, goddesses, preserve me.

3. In midst of whom king Varuṇa is moving,
And looking down surveys men's truth and falsehood:
Who, clear and purifying, drip with sweetness:
Here may those waters, goddesses, preserve me.

4. In whom king Varuṇa, in whom, too, Soma,
In whom the All-gods drink exalted vigour;
Into whom Agni, friend of all, has entered:
Here may those waters, goddesses, preserve me.

APĀṂ NAPĀT

Apāṃ Napāt, the Son of Waters, is invoked in one entire hymn and is often incidentally mentioned elsewhere. He is youthful and brilliant, shining without fuel in the waters that surround and nourish him. Clothed with lightning he is of golden aspect, shining with undimmed splendour in the highest place. He is borne by steeds swift as thought. In the last stanza of the following hymn he is invoked as Agni, who, moreover, is called Apāṃ Napāṭ in an Agni hymn; the epithet, "swiftly-speeding," is further applied to these two deities exclusively, though they are otherwise sometimes distinguished. Apāṃ Napāt thus appears to represent the lightning form of Agni hidden in the cloud. For Agni is not only directly called Apāṃ Napāt, but also described as the "embryo of the waters"; the third form of Agni is, moreover, said to be kindled in the waters.

This god is an inheritance from pre-Indian mythology, for in the *Avesta* Apāṃ Napāṭ is a spirit of the waters who lives in their depths, surrounded by females and often invoked with them, who drives with swift steeds, and is associated with brilliance in the depth of the ocean.

XXIII. SON OF WATERS

II, 35. METRE: TRIṢṬUBH.

1. Desiring gain this eloquence I utter :
May the streams' son accept my songs with gladness.
Will he, the Son of Waters, of swift impulse,
Perchance reward them well ? He will enjoy them.

2. Now from our hearts we would this hymn well-fashioned
Address to him : perchance he will regard it.
The noble Son of Waters, by the greatness
Of rule divine, all creatures has created.

3. Some flow together, some approach the ocean ;
The rivers thus fill up the common cistern.

And him the pure, the shining Son of Waters,
The waters pure on all sides have surrounded.

4. The waters, youthful maidens, never smiling,
Making him bright, encompass him the youthful.
He with clear flames, free-handedly upon us,
Unfed with wood, shines decked with ghee in waters.

5. Three dames divine to him the god, the dauntless,
Wish eagerly to offer food for nurture.
He seems to seek their breasts within the waters:
He drinks the milk of them that first are mothers.

6. The birthplace of this steed is earth and heaven.
Our patrons do thou guard from harm and malice.
Him not to be forgotten, far off dwelling
In cloud-built forts, foes shall not reach nor false-hoods.

7. He in whose house is a productive milch-cow
Increasing vital force, fares on good nurture.
The Waters' Son, expanding in the waters,
Shines forth upon the pious, granting riches.

8. Who in the waters, with celestial brightness,
Shines widely forth, eternal, law-abiding,
Of him as branches every plant and creature
Do propagate themselves with all their offspring.

9. Their son has mounted the lap of the prostrate,
Standing erect and clothed around with lightning.
And bearing on with them his highest greatness,
The swift streams, golden-coloured, flow around him.

10. He is of golden form, of golden aspect,
This Son of Waters is of golden colour.
And him who from a golden birthplace issues,
Those that give gold present with food when seated.

11. That countenance of him, that name belovèd
Of him, the Waters' Son, increase in secret.
Whom thus the maidens all together kindle,
Of him, the golden-hued, the food is butter.

12. Then him the nearest friend of many mortals
We serve with sacrifices, gifts, obeisance.
I make his back to shine, with shavings feed him;
I nourish him with food, with stanzas laud him.

13. He, as a bull, in them that germ engendered;
He, as their infant, sucks their breasts; they kiss him.
He, Son of Waters, of unfading colour,
Here works as with the body of another:

14. While he is dwelling in this highest station,
For ever shining with undimmed effulgence,
The waters bringing ghee to feed their offspring,
Themselves, the swift ones, with their robes fly round him.

15. I have bestowed safe dwelling on our people,
A well-wrought hymn, too, Agni, on our patrons:
All that is favoured by the gods is blessèd.
May we speak loud, with heroes, in the synod.

PṚTHIVĪ: EARTH

The following hymn is the only one in the *Rigveda* to Pṛthivī, Earth, though she is often celebrated with Dyaus, Heaven, conjointly (*e.g.* p. 67), as a dual divinity. There is also a long and beautiful hymn addressed to Pṛthivī in the *Atharvaveda*. The personification is but slight, as the attributes of the goddess are chiefly those of the physical earth. In a funeral hymn she is spoken of as "Kindly mother Earth," and when mentioned with Dyaus she frequently receives the epithet of "Mother." The name means "The broad one," being derived, as indicated in the *Rigveda* itself, from the root *prath*, "To extend."

XXIV. EARTH

V, 84. METRE: ANUṢṬUBH.

1. Thou bearest truly, Pṛthivī,
The burden of the mountains' weight;
With might, O thou of many streams,
Thou quickenest, potent one, the soil.

2. With flowers of speech our songs of praise
Resound to thee, far-spreading one,
Who sendest forth the swelling cloud,
O bright one, like propelling speed;

3. Who, steadfast, holdest with thy might,
The forest-trees upon the ground,
When, from the lightning of thy cloud,
The rain-floods of the sky pour down.

DYĀVĀ-PṚTHIVĪ

Heaven and Earth are the most frequently named pair in the *Rigveda*. They are so closely associated that, while they are invoked as a couple in six hymns, Dyaus, Heaven, is never addressed alone in any hymn, and Pṛthivī, Earth, in only one of three stanzas (p. 66). The two deities are quite co-ordinate, while in most of the other couples, one of the two greatly predominates. Thus they probably represent the prototype of the class of dual divinities in the *Rigveda*.

They are parents besides being separately addressed as "father" and "mother." They have made and sustain all creatures, being also the parents of the gods. One of them is called a prolific bull, the other a varigated cow. They never grow old. Great and far-extended they are broad and vast abodes. They grant food and wealth, bestowing fame and dominion. They are wise and promote righteousness. As parents they guard creatures and protect from disgrace and misfortune. They are sufficiently personified to be called leaders of the sacrifice and to be thought of as seating themselves around the offering; but they never attained to a living personification or importance in worship.

XXV. HEAVEN AND EARTH

I, 185. METRE : TRIṢṬUBH.

1. Which of the two is earlier, which the later?
How were they born, ye sages, who discerns it?
They by themselves support all things existing.
As with a wheel the day and night roll onward.

2. The two support, though moving not and footless,
Abundant offspring having feet and moving.
O Heaven and Earth, from dreadful darkness save us,
Like your own son held in his parents' bosom.

3. I crave of Aditi the gift, the matchless,
Beneficent, illustrious, and honoured:
O ye two worlds, procure that for the singer.
O Heaven and Earth, from dreadful darkness save us.

4. May we be near to both the worlds who suffer
No care, parents of gods, who aid with favour.
Both are divine, with days and nights alternate.
O Heaven and Earth from dreadful darkness save us.

5. Maidens uniting, with adjoining limits,
Twin sisters, resting in their parents' bosom,
They kiss, combined, the universe's centre.
O Heaven and Earth, from dreadful darkness save us.

6. Devoutly I the two seats wide and lofty,
The parents of the gods, invoke with fervour,
Who, fair of aspect, grant us life immortal.
O Heaven and Earth, from dreadful darkness save us.

7. Them wide and broad and great, whose bounds are distant,
Who, beautiful and fain to help, grant blessings:
I at this sacrifice invoke with homage.
O Heaven and Earth, from dreadful darkness save us.

8. If ever we have any sin committed
Against the gods, or friend, or house's chieftain,
Of that may this our hymn be expiation.
O Heaven and Earth, from dreadful darkness save us.

9. May both, as objects of men's praises, bless me;
May both attend me with their help and favour,

Give much to men more liberal than the godless.
We would be strong, ye gods, enjoying nurture.

10. This truth have I now uttered first with wisdom
To Heaven and Earth that every one may hear it.
Protect me from disgrace and peril ; guard me
As Father and as Mother with your succour.

11. May this my prayer come true, O Earth and Heaven,
With which I here address you, Father, Mother.
Be nearest of the gods to us with favours :
May we find food and home with flowing water.

AGNI

Agni and Soma are the two great ritual deities of the *Rigveda*. Judged by the number of hymns addressed to him, Agni is second in importance to Indra (p. 43) only, being invoked in at least 200. His anthropomorphism is only rudimentary, being connected chiefly with the sacrificial aspect of fire. He is butter-backed, flame-haired, has a tawny beard, sharp jaws, and golden teeth. His tongue, with which the gods eat the oblation, is often mentioned. With a burning head he faces in all directions.

Agni is compared with various animals : he resembles a bellowing bull, and sharpens his horns ; when born he is often called a calf ; when kindled he is like a horse that brings the gods, and is yoked to convey the sacrifice to them. He is also a divine bird ; he is the eagle of the sky ; as dwelling in the waters he is like a goose ; he is winged and takes possession of the wood, as a bird perches on a tree.

Wood or ghee is his food, melted butter his drink, and he is nourished three times a day. He is the mouth by which the gods eat the sacrifice ; and his flames are spoons with which he besprinkles the gods ; he is also asked to consume the offerings himself.

Agni's brightness is much dwelt on : he shines like the sun ; his lustre is like the rays of the dawn and the sun, and resembles the lightnings of the rain-cloud. He shines even at night, and dispels the darkness with his beams. On the other hand, his path is black when he invades the forests and shaves the earth as a barber a beard. His flames are like roaring waves, and his sound is like the thunder of heaven. His red smoke rises up to the firmament; like the erector of a post he supports the sky with his smoke. "Smoke-bannered" is his frequent and exclusive epithet. He has a shining, golden, lightning car, drawn by two or more ruddy or tawny steeds. He is the charioteer of sacrifice, and with his steeds he brings the gods on his car. Agni is the child of Heaven, and is often called the son of Heaven and Earth. He is also the offspring of the waters. Indra is called Agni's twin brother, and is more closely associated with him than any other god.

The mythology of Agni, apart from his sacrificial activity, is mostly concerned with his various births, forms and abodes. Mention is often made of his daily production from the two kindling sticks, which are his parents. From the dry wood Agni is born: as soon as born the child devours his parents. The ten fingers of the kindler are called the ten maidens. Owing to the force needed to kindle him, he is spoken of as the "Son of Strength." Being produced every morning, he is young; at the same time no sacrificer is older than he: for he conducted the first sacrifice. Secondly, Agni's origin in the aerial waters is often referred to: he is an embryo of the waters; he is kindled in the waters; he is a bull that has grown in the lap of the waters. As "Son of Waters" (p. 64) he has become a separate deity. He is also sometimes conceived as latent in terrestrial waters. This notion of Agni in the waters is a prominent one in the *Rigveda.* Thirdly, a celestial origin of Agni is often mentioned: he is born in the highest heaven, and was brought down from heaven by Mātariśvan, the Indian Prometheus; and the acquisition of fire by man is regarded as a gift of the gods as well as a production of Mātariśvan. The Sun is, moreover, regarded as a form of Agni. Thus Agni is the light of heaven in the bright sky; he was born on the other side of the air, and sees all things; he is born as the sun rising in the morning. Hence Agni comes to have a triple character: his births are three, or threefold; the gods made him threefold; he is threefold light; he has three heads, three bodies, three stations. The threefold nature of Agni is clearly recognised in the *Rigveda*, and represents the earliest Indian trinity.

The universe being also regarded as consisting of the two divisions of heaven and earth, Agni is said to have two origins, and indeed is the only god described as "having two births." As kindled in numerous dwellings, Agni is said to have many births.

He is more closely associated with human life than any other deity, being the only god called 'Lord of the house" and constantly spoken of as a guest in human dwellings. He is an immortal who has taken up his abode among mortals. Thus he comes to be termed the nearest kinsman of man. He is oftenest described as a father, sometimes also as a brother, or even as a son of his worshippers. He both takes the offerings of men to the gods and brings the gods to the sacrifice. He is thus characteristically a messenger appointed by gods and by men to be an "oblation-bearer."

As the centre of the sacrifice Agni comes to be celebrated as the divine counterpart of the earthly priesthood. Hence he is often called "priest," "domestic priest," and, more often than by any other name, "invoking priest" (*hotar*), less often "officiating priest" and "praying priest." His priesthood is the most salient feature of his character: he is, in fact, the great priest as Indra is the great warrior,

Agni's wisdom is often dwelt upon: as knowing all the details of sacrifice, he is wise and omniscient, being exclusively called "knower of all created beings." He is a great benefactor of his worshippers, bestowing on them all kinds of boons, especially domestic welfare, offspring, and general prosperity. His greatness is often celebrated, being once even said to surpass that of the other gods. His cosmic and creative powers are also frequently praised.

From the ordinary sacrificial Agni, who conveys the offering, is distinguished his "corpse-devouring" form, that burns the body on the funeral pyre. Another function of Agni is to burn and dispel evil spirits and hostile magic.

The sacrificial fire was already in the Indo-Iranian period the centre of a developed ritual, being personified and worshipped as a mighty, wise and beneficent god. It seems to have been an Indo-European institution also, since the Greeks and Romans, as well as the Indians and Iranians, had the custom of offering gifts to the gods in fire. But whether it was already personified in that remote period is a matter of conjecture.

XXVI. AGNI

I, 1. METRE: GĀYATRĪ.

1. Agni I praise, the household priest,
God, minister of sacrifice,
Invoker, best bestowing wealth.

2. Agni is worthy to be praised,
By present as by seers of old:
May he to us conduct the gods.

3. Through Agni may we riches gain,
And day by day prosperity
Replete with fame and manly sons.

4. The worship and the sacrifice,
Guarded by thee on every side,
Go straight, O Agni, to the gods.

5. May Agni, the invoker, wise
And true, of most resplendent fame,
The god, come hither with the gods.

6. Whatever good thou wilt bestow,
O Agni, on the pious man,
That gift comes true, O Angiras.

7. To thee, O Agni, day by day,
O thou illuminer of gloom,
With thought we, bearing homage, come:

8. To thee the lord of sacrifice,
The radiant guardian of the Law,
That growest in thine own abode.

9. So, like a father to his son,
Be easy of approach to us;
Agni, for weal abide with us.

XXVII. AGNI

I, 143. METRE: JAGATĪ; 8 TRIṢṬUBH.

1. A mightier, newer hymn to Agni I present;
My words and song to him, the son of strength, I bring,
Who, offspring of the waters, with bright gods sat down,
As regular and dear invoker, on the earth.

2. As soon as he was in the highest heaven born,
To Mātariśvan Agni manifest became;
As he was kindled, by his might and majesty
His brilliant light illuminated Heaven and Earth.

3. His flames that grow not old, the beams of Agni's fire,
Whose aspect, countenance, and sheen are beautiful,
With mighty radiance undulate and shine afar,
Like glistening rivers' flow: they slumber not nor age.

4. The god, all-knowing Agni, whom the Bhṛgus brought
With might to earth's navel, the centre of the world.
Him stimulate with songs within his own abode,
Who rules, sole sovereign, over wealth, like Varuṇa.

5. Who like the Maruts' roar, or like a dart discharged,
Or like the heavenly bolt can never be restrained:
Agni, the god, with pointed fangs consumes and chews;
He, as a warrior his foes, lays low the woods.

6. Will Agni be a glad receiver of our praise?
   Will he, the bright one, with bright goods grant our desire?
   Will he incite, inspire our thoughts to gain their ends?
   Him of the radiant face now with this song I laud.

7. Who kindles Agni, butter-faced, that draws aloft
   Your sacrifice, he strives to win him as a friend.
   When kindled as a shining banner at our rites,
   May he uplift our radiant-coloured hymn of praise.

8. Incessantly with guards unceasing, Agni,
   That are auspicious and strong, protect us.
   With guards that slumber not, unfailing, watchful,
   Preserve, O helper, all our children safely.

XXVIII. AGNI

VI, 6. METRE : TRIṢṬUBH.

1. The man who seeks success and aid approaches
   The son of strength, with feast and newest worship.
   He rends the wood and has a blackened pathway,
   The brightly radiant and divine invoker.
2. The shining thunderer who dwells in lustre,
   With his unaging, roaring flames, most youthful,
   Refulgent Agni, frequently recurring,
   Goes after many spacious woods and chews them.
3. Thy flames when driven by the wind, O Agni,
   Disperse, O pure one, pure in all directions;
   And thy divine Navagvas, most destructive,
   Lay low the woods and devastate them boldly.
4. Thy steeds, the bright, the pure, O radiant Agni,
   Let loose speed on and shave the ground beneath them.
   Thy whirling flame then widely shines refulgent,
   The highest ridges of earth's surface reaching.
5. When the bull's tongue darts forward like the missile
   Discharged by him who fights the cows to capture,
   Like hero's onset is the flame of Agni:
   Resistless, dreadful, he consumes the forests.

6. Thou with the sunbeams of the great impeller,
Hast boldly overspread the earthly spaces.
So with thy mighty powers drive off all terrors;
Attack our rivals and burn down our foemen.

7. Give us, O splendid one of splendid lordship,
Wealth giving splendour, splendid, life-imparting.
Bestow bright wealth and vast with many heroes,
Bright god, with thy bright flames, upon the singer.

BṚHASPATI

Bṛhaspati is invoked in eleven entire hymns, and in two others conjointly with Indra. His name also appears in the less frequent form of Brahmaṇas pati, Lord of Prayer, the doublets alternating in the same hymn. He is described as sharp-horned and blue-backed, golden-hued and ruddy. He is armed with bow and arrows, and wields a golden hatchet or an iron axe. His car, drawn by ruddy steeds, slays the goblins, bursts open the cow stalls, and wins the light. He is called the father of the gods, and, like Agni, is both a domestic (*purohita*) and a praying priest (*brahman*). Without him, the generator of all prayers, sacrifice does not succeed. His song goes to heaven, and he is associated with singers. He is sometimes identified with Agni, from whom he is, however, much more often distinguished. He is often invoked with Indra, some of whose epithets, such as "wielder of the bolt" and "bountiful," are transferred to him. He is thus drawn into the Indra myth of the release of the cows. Accompanied by his singing host, he rends Vala with a roar, and drives out the cows. In so doing he dispels the darkness and finds the light.

He helps and protects the pious man, prolonging life and removing disease.

The Lord of Prayer seems originally to have represented an aspect of Agni as a divine priest presiding over devotion, an aspect which had already attained an independent character by the beginning of the Rigvedic period. As the divine *brahman* priest he seems to have been the prototype of Brahmā, the chief of the later Hindu trinity.

XXIX. BṚHASPATI

IV, 50. METRE: TRIṢṬUBH; 10 JAGATĪ.

1. Bṛhaspati, in his three seats with thunder
Who mightily has propped apart earth's limits,
Him of the charming tongue, the ancient sages,
Inspired and deeply thinking, placed before them.

2. Bṛhaspati, come from the farthest distance
They, cherishing the rite, for thee are seated.
For thee streams, pressed with stones, and flowing channels,
Distil on all sides mead in great abundance.

4. Bṛhaspati when first he was engendered
From mighty lustre in the highest heaven,
Seven-mouthed and high-born, with his voice of thunder
And seven rays asunder blew the darkness.

5. He with his loudly praising throng of singers
Burst open the enclosing cave with thunder.
Bṛhaspati then drove out, loudly roaring,
The ruddy kine that sweeten the oblation.

6. Him, mighty friend of all the gods, the father,
Serve we with sacrifices, gifts, obeisance.
With goodly offspring and a throng of heroes,
Bṛhaspati, we would be lords of riches.

7. That king indeed by his heroic prowess
And energy defeats all hostile forces,
Who keeps Bṛhaspati well nourished,
Honours and lauds him as the first partaker.

8. He truly in his house dwells well-established,
To him the sacred food affords abundance,
To him his subjects with free will pay homage,
If from this king the priest receives precedence.

9. He unresisted ever wins the riches
Of his own people and surrounding foemen.

The king who to the priest desiring favour
Gives liberty, receives the gods' protection.

10. Bṛhaspati and Indra, ye of mighty wealth,
Drink Soma here, rejoicing at this sacrifice.
May these invigorating drops now enter you :
Bestow on us great wealth and sons exclusively.

11. Bṛhaspati and Indra, make us prosper,
Let that benevolence of yours be with us,
Arouse rewards and give our prayers fulfilment,
The enmities of foes and rivals weaken.

SOMA

As the Soma sacrifice forms the centre of the ritual of the *Rigveda*, this is one of the most prominent deities, coming next in importance to Agni, as indicated by the number of hymns (120) addressed to him. His anthropomorphism is little developed, because the plant and its juice are constantly present to the mind and the vision of the poet.

Soma has sharp and terrible weapons, which he grasps in his hand ; he wields a bow and a thousand-pointed shaft. He has a celestial car drawn by a team like Vāyu's ; he is also said to ride on the same car as Indra ; and he is the best of charioteers. He is associated as a dual divinity in about half a dozen hymns with Indra, Agni, Pūṣan and Rudra. He is sometimes attended by the Maruts, Indra's close allies. He comes to the sacrifice to receive the offerings, and seats himself on the sacred grass.

The intoxicating Soma juice is often called "mead" (*madhu*), but more often the "drop" (*indu*). Its colour is brown, ruddy, or more usually tawny. The whole of the ninth book of the *Rigveda* consists of incantations chanted over the tangible Soma, while its stalks are being pounded by the pressing stones, and the juice, passing through the strainer of sheep's wool, flows into wooden vats, in which it is offered to the gods on the sacred grass. These processes are overlaid with confused and mystical imagery, endlessly varied.

The filtered Soma is mixed with water as well as milk, by which it is sweetened. Soma's connexion with the waters is expressed in many ways. He is the drop that grows in the waters; he is the embryo of the waters or their child; they are his mothers or his sisters; he is lord and king of streams; he produces waters and causes heaven and earth to rain. The sound of the flowing juice is often expressed by verbs meaning to roar, bellow, or even thunder. He is therefore frequently called a bull among the cows (representing the waters). He is, moreover, swift, being often compared with a steed, sometimes with a bird flying to the wood. His yellow colour suggests his brilliance, the physical aspect of Soma on which the poets dwell most frequently. He is then often compared with or associated with the sun.

The exhilarating effect of Soma caused it to be regarded as a drink bestowing immortal life, and to be called the draught of immortality (*amṛta*). All the gods drink Soma; they drank it to gain immortality; it confers immortality not only on the gods, but on men. It also has healing powers, making the blind to see and the lame to walk. As stimulating the voice, Soma is called "Lord of Speech." He awakens eager thought: he is a generator of hymns, a leader of poets, a seer among priests. His wisdom is hence much dwelt on: he is a wise seer, and knows the races of the gods.

The exhilarating powers of Soma are most emphasized in connection with Indra, whom it stimulates for the fight with Vṛtra in innumerable ways. Through this association Indra's warlike exploits come to be attributed to Soma himself: he is a victor unconquered in fight, born for battle; as a warrior he wins all kinds of wealth for his worshippers.

Soma is in several passages said to grow or dwell on the mountains, but his true origin and abode are thought to be in heaven. Soma is the child of heaven, is the milk of heaven, and is purified in heaven; he is the lord of heaven; he occupies heaven, and his place is the highest heaven. Thence he was brought to earth:

the myth embodying this belief is that of the eagle that brings Soma to Indra.

Being the most important of herbs, Soma is said to have been born as the lord of plants, whose king he is; he is the lord of the wood, and has generated all plants.

In a few of the latest hymns of the *Rigveda* Soma begins to be mystically identified with the moon; in the *Atharvaveda* Soma several times means the moon; and in the Brāhmaṇas this identification has already become a commonplace.

The preparation and the offering of Soma (the Avestan *Haoma*) were already an important feature in Indo-Iranian worship. In both the *Rigveda* and the *Avesta* it is said that the Soma stalks were pressed, that its juice was yellow, and was mixed with milk; in both Soma grows on the mountains, though its mythical home is in heaven, whence it comes down to earth; in both Soma has become a mighty god and is called a king; in both there are many other identical mythological traits.

It is possible that the belief in an intoxicating divine beverage, the home of which was in heaven, goes back to the Indo-European period; if so, it must have been regarded as a kind of honey-mead (Sanskrit *mádhu*, Greek *μέθυ*, Anglo-Saxon *medu*).

The name of Soma means "pressed juice," being derived from *su* (avestan *hu*), "to press."

The following hymn does not touch upon the processes of the production of Soma, but dwells on the inspiring, life-giving, remedial, protective, and beneficial powers of the god.

XXX. SOMA

VIII, 48. METRE: TRIṢṬUBH; 5 JAGATĪ.

1. I have partaken wisely of the sweet food
   That stirs good thoughts, best banisher of trouble,
   The food round which all deities and mortals,
   Calling it honey-mead, collect together.

2. Thou shalt be Aditi when thou hast entered
Within, appeaser of celestial anger.
May'st thou, O drop, enjoying Indra's friendship,
Like willing mare the car, to wealth advance us.

3. We have drunk Soma and become immortal;
We have attained the light the gods discovered.
What can hostility now do against us?
And what, immortal god, the spite of mortals?

4. Be cheering to our heart when drunk, O Indu,
Kindly, like father to his son, O Soma.
Like friend for friend, far-famed one, wisely
Prolong our years that we may live, O Soma.

5. These glorious, freedom-giving drops, when drunk
by me,
Have knit my joints together as do thongs a car.
May these protect me now from fracturing a limb.
And may they ever keep me from disease remote.

6. Like fire produced by friction, make me brilliant;
Do thou illumine us and make us richer;
For then I seem in thy carouse, O Soma,
Enriched. Now enter us for real welfare.

7. Of this thy juice pressed out with mind devoted,
We would partake as of paternal riches.
Prolong the years of life for us, King Soma,
As Sūrya lengthens out the days of spring-time.

8. King Soma, gracious be to us for welfare:
We are thy devotees; of that be mindful.
O Indu, might and anger rise against us:
Hand us not over to our foeman's mercies.

9. Thou, as the guardian of our body, Soma,
Surveying men, in every limb hast settled.
If we perchance infringed, O god, thy statutes,
As our good friend for greater wealth be gracious.

10. I would accompany the friend, the wholesome,
Who, Lord of Bays, imbibed, would never hurt me.
I come to Indra to prolong our life-time,
That we may relish Soma placed within us.

11. Away have fled those ailments and diseases;
The powers of darkness have been all affrighted.
With mighty strength in us has Soma mounted:
We have arrived where men prolong existence.

12. The drop drunk deeply in our hearts, O Fathers,
Us mortals that immortal god has entered.
That Soma we would worship with oblation;
We would be in his mercy and good graces.

13. Uniting with the Fathers thou, O Soma,
Hast over Heaven and Earth thyself extended.
So, Indu, we would serve thee with oblation:
Thus we would be the lords of ample riches.

14. Do ye, protecting gods, speak in our favour,
Let neither sleep nor idle talk subdue us;
May we, for evermore, beloved of Soma,
Endowed with hero sons, address the synod.

15. Thou, Soma, givest strength to us on all sides.
Light-finder, watching men, within us enter.
Do thou, O Indu, with thine aids accordant,
Behind for ever and before protect us.

ARAṆYĀNĪ

The following is the only hymn of the *Rigveda* in which Araṇyānī, the goddess of the Forest, is invoked. Here the various sounds heard in her dark solitudes at nightfall are weirdly described.

XXXI. ARAṆYĀNĪ

X, 146. METRE: ANUṢṬUBH.

1. O forest nymph, O forest nymph,
Thou seemest to have lost thy way:
Why dost not for the village ask?
Has fear, perchance, now entered thee?

2. When to the owl's loud-sounding hoot
The parrot makes an answering cry,
And hops, as to the cymbal's clash,
Then Araṇyānī heaves with joy.

3. Sounds as of cows that graze are heard,
A dwelling house appears to loom,
And Araṇyānī, forest nymph,
Creaks like a cart at eventide.

4. Here some one calls his cow to him,
Another there is felling wood :
Who in the forest bides at eve
Thinks to himself, "I heard a cry."

5. Never does Araṇyānī hurt,
Unless one goes too near to her ;
When she has eaten of sweet fruit,
At her own will she goes to rest.

6. Sweet-scented, redolent of balm,
Replete with food, though tilling not,
Mother of beasts, the forest nymph,
Her I have magnified with praise.

WEDDING HYMN

Among the hymns not directly addressed to the gods, but rather coming within the sphere of social life, is the wedding hymn. As, however, social usages were dominated by religion, the poem has a religious and mythological colouring. It is of great length, consisting of 47 stanzas, and lacking poetical unity. It contains groups of stanzas relating to the marriage ceremonial loosely strung together. The following stanzas have been selected from it as the most suitable for translation in this volume. The poem begins (1-5) with mystical identification of the celestial Soma with the moon; then follow (6-17) stanzas relating to the wedding of Soma, the moon, with the Sun-maiden, Sūrya. The sun and moon are next described as an inseparable pair (18-19).

XXXII. WEDDING HYMN

X, 85. METRE : 18, 44, JAGATĪ ;
19, 26, 27, 36, TRIṢṬUBH ;
31, 32, 38, 42, 47, GĀYATRĪ.

18. These two speed on with mystic power alternately ;
Like playful children they go round the sacrifice.

One of the two surveys the whole created world ;
The other, seasons meting out, is born again.

19. Ever anew, being born again, he rises ;
He goes before the dawns as daylight's token.
He, coming, to the gods their share apportions :
The moon draws out the span of man's existence.

Blessings are then invoked on the wedding procession, and good wishes expressed for the future of the newly-married couple (20-33):

26. Let Pūṣan lead thee home, thy hand well grasping,
And let the Aśvins on their chariot drive thee.
Go to thy home that thou may'st be its mistress,
And with authority address the synod.

27. May fortune here with offspring be thy portion,
In this abode be of thine household watchful.
And with thine husband here be thou united ;
And till old age do ye address the synod.

. . . . . .

31. The ailments, coming from her kin,
That her bright wedding throng pursue,
These may the holy gods drive back,
Towards the place from which they came.

32. May those who lie in wait around
Their path, not find the bridal pair ;
May these by easy roads escape
The peril ; may their foes disperse.

The two next stanzas (34-35), which contain some obscure references to the bridal garments, are followed by six others (36-41) pronounced at the wedding rite, which is again brought into relation with the marriage of Sūryā. The bridegroom here first addresses the bride, and then Agni, as the god of the nuptial fire, is invoked :

36. I grasp thy hand that I may gain good fortune,
That thou may'st reach old age with me as husband.
Aryaman, Bhaga, Savitar, Puraṃdhi,
The gods, give thee to me for life domestic.

. . . .

38. For thee they first drove Sūryā home
Together with the wedding throng:
O Agni, to her spouse give back
His wife, and to her offspring grant.

The concluding stanzas (42-47) are benedictions pronounced on the newly-wedded pair, after the arrival of the bride at her future home:

42. Abide ye here; be not disjoined;
Complete life's full allotted span,
Frolicking with sons and grandsons,
Rejoicing in your own abode.

. . . . . .

44. Free from the evil eye, thy husband hurting not,
Kind to our beasts, be friendly, full of energy;
Bear heroes, love the gods, and live in happiness;
Bring welfare to our bipeds and our quadrupeds.

. . . . . .

47. May all the gods unite our hearts,
And may the Waters them entwine;
May Mātariśvan and Dhātar,
May Deṣṭrī them together join.

FUNERAL HYMNS

The following two hymns belong to the group of five (x, 14-18) dealing with death and the future life. From these we learn that, though burial was also practised, cremation was the normal method of disposing of the dead, and formed the basis of the mythology relating to the future life. Agni conveys the corpse to the other world, the Fathers, and the gods. He is besought to preserve the body intact, and to burn the goat that is sacrificed as his portion. The way to the heavenly world is by a distant path, on which Savitar conducts and Pūṣan protects the dead. Before the pyre is lighted, the wife of the dead man, having lain beside him, arises, and his bow is taken from his hand. This indicates that in earlier times his widow and his weapons were burnt with the body of the husband.

Passing along the path trodden by the Fathers, the spirit of the deceased goes to the realm of light, and meets the Fathers who revel with Yama in the highest heaven. Here, united with a glorious body, he enters upon a life of bliss which is free from imperfections and bodily frailties, in which all desires are fulfilled, and which is passed among the gods, especially the two kings, Yama and Varuṇa.

XXXIII. THE WAY TO YAMA'S REALM

X, 14. METRE: TRIṢṬUBH; 13-14 ANUṢṬUBH; 15 BṚHATĪ.

1. Him who has past along the mighty ridges,
   And has spied out the path for many travellers,
   Vivasvant's son, the gatherer of people,
   Yama, the king, do thou present with offering.

2. For us has Yama first found out the pathway:
   This pasture never can be taken from us.
   To where have passed away our former fathers,
   The later born by their own paths have travelled.

4. Upon this sacred grass sit down, O Yama,
   Uniting with the Aṅgiras, our fathers.
   Let spells recited by the sages bring thee;
   Do thou, O king, rejoice in this oblation.

5. Come hither with the Aṅgiras, the holy:
   Here with Virūpa's sons, O Yama revel,
   Vivasvant I invoke, who is thy father,
   When at this rite upon the straw he's seated.

6. The Aṅgiras, our fathers, the Navagvas,
   The Bhṛgus and Atharvans, Soma-loving:
   May we abide for ever in the favour
   And the good graces of those holy sages.

7. Depart, depart, along those ancient pathways,
   On which have passed away our former fathers:
   There thou shalt see rejoicing in libations
   The two kings, Varuṇa the god and Yama.

8. Unite thou with the Fathers and with Yama,
   With thy good works' reward in highest heaven.

To home return, all imperfection leaving.
Unite with thine own body, full of vigour.

9. Begone, depart from here, disperse and scatter:
For him the Fathers have prepared this dwelling.
Yama bestows on him this place to rest in,
A place by waters, days and nights distinguished.

10. Run on thy path straight forward, past the two dogs,
The sons of Saramā, four-eyed and brindled.
Draw near thereafter to the bounteous Fathers,
Who revel on in company with Yama.

11. O King, to those two this dead man deliver,
The two that are thy guardian dogs, O Yama,
Four-eyed, observing men, the pathway watching.
Bestow upon the dead man health and welfare.

12. Broad-nosed and brown the messengers of Yama,
Greedy of lives they rove among the people.
May they give back to us a life propitious
Here and to-day, that we may see the sunlight.

13. For Yama press the Soma juice,
To Yama offering present.
To Yama goes the sacrifice,
Announced by Agni, well-prepared.

14. To Yama offering rich in ghee
Present forthwith, and forward step.
Let him direct us to the gods,
That we may live a life prolonged.

15. To Yama as a King present
Oblation very honey-sweet.
This homage is for seers of old,
The ancient makers of the path.

XXXIV. FUNERAL PRAYER

X, 18. METRE: TRIṢṬUBH; 11 PRASTĀRAPAṄKTI; 13 JAGATĪ.

1. Depart, O Death, along the farthest pathway,
Which is thine own, not that by mortals trodden.
I speak to thee that hast both eyes and hearing:
Do not our offspring injure nor our heroes.

2. Since ye have come, the trace of death effacing,
Till future days prolonging your existence :
With offspring and with riches thriving greatly,
Do ye, O pious men, be pure and holy.

3. These living men have from the dead been parted;
Our calling of the gods is now auspicious.
We have come near, prepared for dance and laughter,
Till future days prolonging our existence.

4. For those that live do I set up this limit,
May now no other one this goal encounter.
May they exist a hundred ample autumns :
By this stone may they death remove far from them.

5. As days in order follow one another,
As seasons duly alternate with seasons,
And as the later ne'er forsakes the earlier,
So settle thou the lives of these, Ordainer.

6. Do ye attain long life, old age selecting,
As many as you are combined in order.
May Tvaṣṭar, well-disposed, the skilled creator,
Produce forthwith long life for your existence.

7. These women here, non-widows, with good husbands,
Let them provide themselves with fat and butter.
Tearless and free from care, well-decked with jewels,
Let first these wives ascend the place of mourning.

8. Arise, come to the world of life, O woman;
Thou liest here by one whose breath has left him.
Come: thou hast entered upon the wifehood
Of this thy lord who takes thy hand and woos thee.

9. From the dead hand I take the bow he wielded,
To win for us dominion, might, and glory.
Thou there, we here, rich in heroic offspring,
Will vanquish all assaults of every foeman.

10. Approach the bosom of the earth, the mother,
This earth, the far-extending, most propitious;
Young, soft as wool to bounteous givers, may she
Preserve thee from the lap of dissolution.

11. Wide open, earth, O press not heavily on him;
Be easy of approach to him, a refuge safe;
As with a robe a mother hides
Her son, so shroud this man, O earth.

12. Now opening wide may here the earth stand stead-
fast,
May here a thousand columns rise to prop her;
May here those mansions ever drip with butter,
And here be always shelter to protect him.

13. For thee I now prop up the earth around thee here;
In lowering this clod may I receive no harm.
May the Fathers hold up for thee this column,
And Yama here provide for thee fit mansions.

THE GAMBLER

The following is one of a small group among the secular hymns which have a didactic character. It is the comment of a gambler, who, unable to resist the fascination of the dice, deplores the ruin he has brought on himself and his household. The dice consisted of the nuts of a large tree, called *Vibhīdaka*, still used for this purpose in India.

XXXV. THE GAMBLER

X, 34. METRE: TRIṢṬUBH; 7 JAGATĪ.

1. On high trees born and in a windy region
The danglers, rolling on the diceboard, cheer me.
Like Soma draught from Mūjavant's great mountain,
The rousing nut Vibhīdaka has pleased me.

2. She wrangles not with me nor is she angry:
To me and comrades she was ever kindly.
For dice that only luckless throws effected
I've driven away from home a wife devoted.

3. Her mother hates me, she herself rejects me:
For one in such distress there is no pity.
I find a gambling man is no more useful
Than is an aged horse that's in the market.

4. Others embrace the wife of him whose chattels
The eager dice have striven hard to capture;
And father, mother, brothers say about him:
"We know him not; lead him away a captive."

5. When to myself I think, "I'll not go with them,
I'll stay behind my friends that go to gamble,"
And those brown nuts, thrown down, have raised their voices,
I go, like wench, straight to the place of meeting.

6. To the assembly hall the gambler sallies,
And asking, "Shall I win?" he quakes and trembles.
And then the dice run counter to his wishes,
Giving the lucky throw to his opponent.

7. The dice attract the gambler, but deceive and wound,
Both paining men at play and causing them to pain.
Like boys they offer first and then take back their gifts:
With honey sweet to gamblers by their magic charm.

8. Their throng in triple fifties plays untrammelled,
Like Savitar the god whose laws are constant.
They yield not to the wrath of even the mighty:
A king himself on them bestows obeisance.

9. Downward they roll, then swifty springing upward,
They overcome the man with hands, though handless.
Cast on the board like magic bits of charcoal,
Though cold themselves, they burn the heart to ashes.

10. Grieved is the gambler's wife by him abandoned,
Grieved, too, his mother as he aimless wanders.
Indebted, fearing, he desiring money
At night approaches other people's houses.

11. It pains the gambler when he sees a woman
Another's wife, and their well-ordered household.
He yokes those brown steeds early in the morning,
And when the fire is low sinks down a beggar.

12. To him who's general of your mighty forces,
As king becomes the chief of your battalions,
I hold my fingers ten extended forward:
"No money I withhold, this truth I tell thee."

13. Play not with dice, but cultivate thy tillage,
Enjoy thy riches, deeming them abundant.
There are thy cows, there is thy wife, O Gambler:
This counsel Savitar the noble gives me.

14. Make friends with us, we pray, to us be gracious;
Do not bewitch us forcibly with magic;
Let now your enmity, your anger slumber:
Let others be in brownies' toils entangled.

THE PURSUIT OF GAIN

The following hymn, originally a popular poem, has by means of a refrain (here omitted) been drawn into the Soma cult. It describes with mild humour how men seek wealth in various ways.

XXXVI. THE PURSUIT OF GAIN

IX, 112. METRE: ANUṢṬUBH.

1. Various indeed are our concerns,
And men's vocations manifold:
The carpenter and leech desire
A break; the priest a Soma rite.

2. The smith, with dry wood on his hearth,
With wings of birds to fan the fire,
With anvil and with glowing flames,
Desires a patron rich in gold.

3. A poet I: my dad's a leech,
Mama the upper millstone turns:
With various aims we strive for wealth,
As if we followed after kine.

SPEECH

This hymn deals with wise, sacred speech as that of the Veda and of Brahmins, not that of men in general.

XXXVII. HYMN TO SPEECH

X, 71. METRE: TRIṢṬUBH ; 9 JAGATĪ.

1. When seers, Bṛhaspati, in early ages,
Assigning names, of speech the first sounds uttered,
Then was revealed their best unsoiled possession
That hidden in their hearts with love they cherished.

2. Where wise men fashion speech with understanding
And sift it, as with sieves the corn is winnowed,
There friends may learn to know each other's friendship:
Upon their speech is set the stamp of beauty.

3. The track of speech with sacrifice they followed,
And found it in the midst of sages lurking;
They took and scattered it in many places:
The seven singers chanted it in chorus.

4. And many a one, though seeing, does not grasp it,
While others, though they hear, have no cognition.
But speech to many a one surrenders freely,
As wife, fair-robed and willing, to her husband.

5. They say that many a man has grown in friendship
Both stiff and stout: they send him not to contests,
He with illusion unprolific wanders:
The speech he's learnt yields neither fruit nor blossom.

6. Whoever his devoted friend abandons,
In speech for him there's no participation,
And what he hears, he hears without perception;
For such a man knows not the path of virtue.

7. Though having eyes and ears alike, companions
Appear unequal in their mental quickness.
Some are like lakes that reach to mouth or armpits,
While others seem like shallow ponds for bathing.

8. When, having in their hearts gained mental quickness,
The Brahmins sacrifice as friends together,
Then many a one is left behind in knowledge,
While others stride in front with prayers effective.

9. Those men who do not hurry here and there with zeal,
Who are not Brahmins nor press out the Soma juice,
They having gained, to no good end, the power of speech,
As unproductive workers weave their web in vain.

10. All friends rejoice when their companion famous
Returns from the assembly hall a victor.
He drives away reproach and wins them nurture :
He is sent out as fitted for the contest.

11. The one sits putting forth rich bloom of stanzas ;
Another sings a song in skilful metres ;
A third as Brahmin states the laws of being ;
A fourth metes out the sacrifice's measure.

XXXVIII. IN PRAISE OF CHARITY

X, 117. METRE: TRIṢṬUBH ; 1-2 JAGATĪ.

1. The gods inflict not hunger as a means to kill :
Death frequently befalls even satiated men.
The charitable giver's wealth melts not away ;
The niggard never finds a man to pity him.

2. Who, of abundant food possessed, makes hard his heart
Towards a needy and decrepit suppliant
Whom once he courted, come to pray to him for bread :
A man like this as well finds none to pity him.

3. He is the liberal man who helps the beggar
That, craving food, emaciated wanders,
And coming to his aid, when asked to succour,
Immediately makes him a friend hereafter.

4. He is no friend who gives not of his substance
To his devoted, intimate companion :

This friend should turn from him—here is no haven—
And seek a stranger elsewhere as a helper.

5. The wealthier man should give unto the needy,
Considering the course of life hereafter;
For riches are like chariot wheels revolving:
Now to one man they come, now to another.

6. The foolish man from food has no advantage;
In truth I say: it is but his undoing;
No friend he ever fosters, no companion:
He eats alone, and he alone is guilty.

7. The plough that cleaves the soil produces nurture;
He that bestirs his feet completes his journey.
The speaking Brahmin earns more than the silent;
A friend who gives is better than the niggard.

8. The one-foot[1] strides more swiftly than the biped;[2]
The biped goes beyond him who has three feet.[3]
The quadruped[4] comes at the call of bipeds,
And watches near where groups of five are gathered.

9. Two hands though equal make not what is equal;
No sister cows yield milk in equal measure;
Unequal is the strength even of twin children;
The gifts of even kinsmen are unequal.

SARAMĀ AND THE PAṆIS

The following hymn is a good specimen of a mythical dialogue, of which type there are several examples in the *Rigveda*. It belongs to the myth of the capture by Indra of the cows of the Paṇis, demons who keep herds of cattle in a cave far away beyond the Rasā, a mythical river. It is a colloquy in alternate stanzas between the Paṇis and Saramā, Indra's female messenger, who tracks the cows and asks for them in Indra's name, but is mocked by the demons. The final stanza is spoken by the poet, who, repeating the last words of

[1] The Sun. [2] Man. [3] Old man with a staff. [4] Dog.

Saramā, apostrophises the Paṇis to abandon the cows because they are destined to be captured. In the last two lines he indicates that the capture was effected by Indra's ally, Bṛhaspati (p. 75), in association with Soma, who stimulates to such deeds, and with the pressing stones by which Soma is produced.

XXXIX. SARAMĀ AND THE PAṆIS

X, 108. METRE: TRIṢṬUBH.

1. With what desire has Saramā come hither?
For weary is the way and far the distance.
What was for us the message, what her roaming?
How didst thou pass across the Rasā's waters?

2. I come sent out as messenger by Indra,
O Paṇis, searching round for your great treasures.
In fear that I should leap across, she helped me:
I traversed thus the waters of the Rasā.

3. What, Saramā, is Indra like, as envoy
For whom thou comest from the farthest distance?
Let him come here: we will make him our comrade.
So let him be the herdsman of our cattle.

4. I know he can't be harmed, but injures others,
He as whose envoy from afar I come here.
Deep-flowing streams cannot conceal his body:
By Indra slain, ye shall lie prostrate, Paṇis.

5. Those cows for which, O Saramā, thou soughtest,
Around the ends of heaven flying, fair one:
Who them to thee would leave without resistance?
And sharp indeed our weapons are in conflict.

6. Though these your words can not be fought with missiles,
Nor those mis-shapen bodies pierced by arrows,
Nor yet the road be forced, to reach your stronghold:
Bṛhaspati will never spare you, Paṇis.

7. This treasure, Saramā, on rock is founded,
Replete with goods, and cows, and horses.

The Paṇis here, its stout protectors, guard it:
In vain thou comest to a fort unyielding.

8. Hither will come the seers inspired with Soma,
Ayāsya, Aṅgirases, and Navagvas:
They will appropriate this stall of cattle.
The Paṇis then shall all these boasts relinquish.

9. And since, O Saramā, thus by compulsion
Divine coerced, thou hast come hither to us:
We will make thee our sister: pray return not;
We will give thee a share of kine, thou fair one.

10. I know not what's a brother or a sister:
The fierce Aṅgirases and Indra know it.
They seemed to me, when I came here, right eager
For kine: from hence go far away, ye Paṇis.

11. Go, Paṇis, to the distance far: the cattle
Shall issue, breaking rightly from their prison.
Bṛhaspati, the pressing stones, and Soma,
And priestly sages found them in concealment.

FROG HYMN

The following hymn, intended as a rain-producing spell, is a panegyric of frogs, which are compared during the drought to heated sacrificial vessels, and are described as raising their voices together at the commencement of the rains, like Brahmin pupils repeating the lessons of their teacher.

XL. FROGS

VII, 103. METRE: TRIṢṬUBH; 1 ANUṢṬUBH.

1. Resting in silence for a year,
Like Brahmins practising a vow,
The frogs have lifted up their voices,
Excited by Parjanya's call.

2. When heavenly waters have poured down upon them
Resting in pools, like dried up leather buckets,
The croakings of the frogs resound together,
Like noise of cows with calves in concert lowing.

3. When showers have streamed around them, eager, thirsty,
Upon the advent of the rainy season,
With joyful croak the one draws near the other
Who greets him, as a son comes near his father.

4. The one of them the other hails with welcome,
When in the flow of waters they have revelled;
When rained upon the frogs become exultant,
He that is Spotty joins his voice to Tawny's.

5. When one repeats the utterance of the other,
As those who learn the lessons of their teacher,
All this is like concordant recitation,
As eloquent ye prate upon the waters.

6. One lows like cows, one like a goat is bleating;
This one is Spotty, one of them is Tawny.
Bearing a common name they're many-coloured,
They variously adorn their voice in speaking.

7. As Brahmins at the mighty Soma offering
Sit round the large and brimming vessel talking;
So throng ye all around the pool to hallow
This annual day that, frogs, begins the rain-time.

8. These Soma-pressing Brahmins raise their voices
And offer their recurrent year's devotion;
And these Adhvaryu priests with kettles sweating
Come forth to view, and none of them are hidden.

9. The twelve months' god-sent order they have guarded,
And never do these men infringe the season.
When in the year the rainy time commences,
Those who were heated milk-pots gain deliverance.

10. Both Lowing Cow and Bleating Goat have given,
Spotty and Tawny, too, have given us riches.
The frogs give kine by hundreds; they for pressings
Of Soma thousandfold, prolong existence.

INDEX